Greenberg's Guide to
LIONEL TRAINS
1945-1969

Volume IV
Uncatalogued Sets

Paul V. Ambrose
and
Joseph P. Algozzini

Greenberg Publishing Company, Inc.
Sykesville, Maryland

Greenberg Publishing Company, Inc.
7566 Main Street
Sykesville, Maryland 21784
(410) 795-7447

First Edition

Manufactured in the United States of America

Greenberg Publishing Company, Inc. publishes the world's largest selection of Lionel, American Flyer, LGB, Marx, Ives, and other toy train publications as well as a selection of books on model and prototype railroading, dollhouse building, and collectible toys. For a complete listing of current Greenberg publications, please call 1-800-533-6644 or write to Kalmbach Publishing, 21027 Crossroads Circle, Waukesha, Wisconsin 53187.

Greenberg Shows, Inc. sponsors *Greenberg's Great Train, Dollhouse and Toy Shows*, the world's largest of its kind. The shows feature extravagant operating train layouts, and a display of magnificent dollhouses. The shows also present a huge marketplace of model and toy trains, for HO, N, and Z Scales; Lionel O and Standard Gauges; and S and 1 Gauges; plus layout accessories and railroadiana. They also offer a large selection of dollhouse miniatures and building materials, and collectible toys. Shows are scheduled along the East Coast each year from Massachusetts to Florida. For a list of our current shows please call (410) 795-7447 or write to Greenberg Shows, Inc., 7566 Main Street, Sykesville, Maryland 21784 and request a show brochure.

Greenberg Auctions, a division of Greenberg Shows, Inc., offers nationally advertised auctions of toy trains and toys. Please contact our auction manager at (410) 795-7447 for further information.

ISBN 0-89778-287-9 (Hardback)
ISBN 0-89778-282-8 (Softback)

Library of Congress Cataloging-in-Publication Data
(Revised for vol. 4)

Greenberg, Bruce C.
    Greenberg's guide to Lionel trains, 1945-1969.

    Vol. 1 edited by Paul V. Ambrose; v. 2 by Dallas J.
Mallerich III and Marcy Damon.
    Vol. 1: 8th ed.; v. 2: 2nd ed.; v. 3: 1st ed.;
v. 4: 1st ed.

    Vol. 3 published in 1990.
    Errata slips inserted in v. 1-2.
    Includes indexes.
    Contents: v. 1. Motive power and rolling stock,
including accessories — v. 2. Behind the
scenes — v. 3. Sets — v. 4. Uncatalogued sets / by
Paul V. Ambrose and Joseph P. Algozzini.

    1. Railroads—Models. 2. Lionel Corporation.
I. Ambrose, Paul V. II. Guide to Lionel trains,
1945-1969. III. Title.
TF197.G667 1991   625.1'9   90-23177
    ISBN 0-89778-282-8 (v. 4 : soft cover)
    ISBN 0-89778-287-9 (v. 4 : hard cover)

CONTENTS

PROLOGUE 6

COLLECTING UNCATALOGUED SETS 16

SEARS, ROEBUCK AND CO. The Goliath from Chicago 21

MONTGOMERY WARD Another Midwestern Giant 43

SPIEGEL Chicago's Other Participant 49

J. C. PENNEY The East Coast Connection 56

FIRESTONE A Train Stop in Ohio 65

GENERAL RETAILERS What the Rest of America Had to Offer 68

GLOSSARY 123

INDEX 127

Dedication

*To my children Bryan and Amanda: older son and a young daughter
who make me proud to be called "Dad."*

A continuing thank you is extended to **Bob Morgan** and **Ed Prendeville** of Train Collector's Warehouse for always opening their doors to us, and to **David Cirillo**, **Harry Lovelock**, and **Fred Davis** for valuable information they so graciously furnished. We also thank **V. Bibelot**, **S. Bradley**, **B. Myles**, and **M. Sokol** for allowing us to photograph portions of their collections.

Robert Swanson graciously took the time to review major portions of the manuscript, and we appreciate his willingness to share his expertise. His comments were most helpful. Thanks also to **I. D. Smith** for forwarding pertinent information.

We also thank the following collectors for providing information on various sets: **T. Austern**, **D. Bauer**, **W. Grimes**, **P. Iurilli**, **D. Jackson**, **J. Kerr**, **T. Klaassen**, **R. Larson**, **G. Ligon**, **G. Metelak**, **D. Miller**, **R. Okun**, **D. Pickard**, **W. Pike**, **A. Stewart**, **W. Stitt**, **C. Swanson**, and **F. Wasserman**.

At the top of the list of "thank yous" for in-house Greenberg staff is **Barbara Morey**. Although she is not a Lionel sage, I am most grateful to her for the time, energy, and technical expertise expended on this book. She toiled with me on a daily basis for nearly a year, maintaining the most up-beat and pleasant of dispositions. She has been a joy to work with. Thank you to **Donna Price** for her careful proofreading of the manuscript, and to **Samuel Baum** who provided overall support to the project. Also, thanks to Senior Artist **Maureen Crum** for her work on the cover design and color photos, Graphic Artist **Wendy Burgio** for the book layout and graphics, and **Brian Falkner**, Graphic Arts department manager. **Bruce C. Greenberg**, with the assistance of **Brad Schwab**, took most of the photographs for this book; the photograph on page 58 was taken by **A. L. Schmidt**, Kalmbach Publishing Co.

Paul V. Ambrose
February 1992

Dedication

*To my parents, with sincere gratitude for giving me that first train set in 1948,
which has been instrumental in directing me toward my lifetime
ambition of collecting and researching postwar Lionel trains.*

Special thanks to all the collectors who have helped me compile information on uncatalogued sets over the years, and especially to those individuals who entrusted me with their sets or other materials to be photographed for this first edition. They include **Bob Bretch, Ed Dougherty, Carl** and **Charles Hurschik, Rich Mack, Mel Nicholas, Ernie Reising, Bob Sylvan, Mike Toth, Bill Vasilion, John White,** and the **American Heritage Center,** University of Wyoming. Thanks also to the archive departments of **J. C. Penney; Sears, Roebuck and Co.;** and **Speigel.**

We would also like to thank the following collectors for the information they gave us regarding their sets. They include **J. Amanda, W. Corsello, R. Corruthers, R. Hall, D. Julio, D. LeGore, M. McFadden, P. Michael, T. Michels, R. Scott, R. Stepan, R. Thomas, A. Tolli, L. Vasilion, C. Vegazo, M. Visnick,** and **T. Vittorio.**

Joseph P. Algozzini
February 1992

PROLOGUE

This book explores uncharted seas and is based primarily on the authors' first-hand information on uncatalogued sets obtained through their years of collecting postwar Lionel trains. Secondary information was taken from advertisements, catalogues of major retailers such as Sears and J. C. Penney, and input of other members of the collecting community. Unfortunately, Lionel has not left us (or we have not yet uncovered) the necessary documentation to completely chronicle the history of promotional or uncatalogued sets. Very little Lionel data survives. Production records and outfit information may have been "circular filed" as the years went by. Computer use was in its infancy, and at the time, the most pertinent records for Lionel to keep were payroll data and tax information.

Assessing Value

The less expensive Lionel uncatalogued and promotional sets have been neglected in previous research on toy trains; this is unfortunate, since many of these sets represent some of Lionel's most creative and important marketing efforts. One must remember that during Lionel's reign as America's most noted maker of toy trains, the trains of Louis Marx continually threatened the low end of Lionel's pricing structure, and Lionel's marketing creativity was sorely tested. These low-end sets were the means by which many a boy was introduced to Lionel. Because of low pricing and stiff competition, Lionel put special efforts into the engineering of these sets because, quite literally, pennies counted!

Many uncatalogued Lionel sets have been dismissed by collectors as "junk" all too often, but before the collector assails Lionel for making "cheap" trains, he should recognize the place these trains held in Lionel's marketing strategy. It is highly unlikely that The Lionel Corporation would have survived as long as it did if it had to rely solely on its catalogued and more expensive trains. Fortunately, in recent years there has been increasing interest in uncatalogued sets.

Marketing Direction

Uncatalogued/promotional sets served many purposes. First and foremost, they brought extra customers into the Lionel showroom. They also afforded their full-price customers the opportunity to purchase merchandise with a break on price at season's end. By purchasing merchandise with a lower cost price, the retailer had more "water" in his mark-up. Subsequently, the retailer had more latitude to mark down suggested retail prices and still retain an acceptable profit margin. (Promotional buying such as this is prevalent in the retail industry. It was and is done every day of the week on any item imaginable; it is the American way.) Of equal importance, promotional sets enabled Lionel to deplete unsold, overstocked merchandise and to keep their inventory current. When they were desperate to move merchandise, whether sets or single items, Lionel would call an "undertaker" as a last resort. An undertaker is a merchant who buys "dead" inventory. One of the most notable undertakers was the original Madison Hardware, formerly located on 23rd Street in New York City; they bought anything if the price was right.

Uncatalogued sets were initially directed to major retailers or national distributors such as Sears, Macy's, Firestone, and Western Auto. Pre-1956 outfits, for the most part, were the same as catalogued sets and were comprised of standard production engines and rolling stock. In order to provide the individual retailer with something unique, outfits were often assembled, beginning in 1955, with rosters different from those shown in the consumer catalogue. Lionel was able to glamorize the contents by sometimes adding extra track and items such as low-cost Plasticville and trestle sets that took up space in the box and made the set appear more impressive than it actually was. Some of the miscellaneous items that Lionel included in their uncatalogued sets would defy belief if their contents were not listed on the outside of the set carton.

To some customers, Lionel also offered outfits that were identical in content to its catalogued sets; however, these sets were numbered differently from the catalogued sequence. For example, 1956 catalogued set 1547S headed by a 2018 steam engine was also sold in the same box and packaged in the same manner as set 149 to Gifts Galore and as set 11-L-42 to Firestone. Other examples of catalogued sets appearing with uncatalogued outfit numbers are documented throughout the text.

The uncatalogued/promotional sets with their deceptive outfit numbers protected both Lionel and their full-price wholesale customers. For example, a hobby shop owner who wrote orders at "line price" could get exceedingly upset (and with reason) if the set for which he paid the purchase order price and retailed at Lionel's suggested price appeared for less money in a discount store. Better full-price, full-service retailers wanted (and still do) to distance themselves from discounters whom they felt might taint their "better" name or the image for which they strove.

As time progressed, the uncatalogued sets became more of a factor in Lionel's marketing strategy. Lionel solicited business from large national brand food companies, such as Quaker Oats and Libby, as well as manufacturers of household necessities, and made them special sets that sometimes included a promotional car. This practice actually began in the late 1950s with sets that contained the 6014 Chun King, 6024 RCA Whirlpool, and the 6014-150 W I X Filters boxcar.

The mid-1960s was a low point in Lionel's history. Train sales during the period were so dismal that Lionel did anything it could to generate business. Lionel train sets appeared in previously shunned dime stores such as F. W. Woolworth, G. C. Murphy and similar low-end establishments; although he was retired, Joshua Lionel Cowen's blood pressure probably rose to new heights. The Company would sell to anybody who came into the showroom as long as they were creditworthy. It was in a struggle for its existence; timely payments and profitability were the sole determining factors as to who got what merchandise and at what time.

Product Authenticity

One major tenet must be stressed—*Know Thy Product!* Many uncatalogued "sets" offered in the toy train market are nothing more than some trains in a box! A set, to be a set, must be correct in every aspect, i.e., it must contain properly dated items, correct trucks, component boxes where applicable, etc. Regrettably, most purported sets are not. Because many of these uncatalogued sets were intended for first-time buyers rather than collectors, they usually ended up in the hands of children who *played* with them. When they are offered in the marketplace, they are often incomplete and usually in less than collector condition.

A promotional set box has often been "a license to create," since neither sellers nor buyers have had a standard reference as to what the set should contain. Many

either incomplete or empty original outfit boxes have been filled with various engines and rolling stock by both collectors and dealers, with little attention paid to accuracy, just to facilitate the sale of inventory. The standard answer to any probing question from a prospective purchaser is "Well, that's the way I got it." Some sellers become immediately confrontational, with a take-it-or-leave-it attitude when questioned about an outfit with "suspect" contents. The authors suggest following a simple policy: When in doubt, walk away, or barter for an appropriate price reduction.

There is no substitute for knowledge; it enables collectors to determine whether an outfit is factory-correct or an after-the-fact put-together. Keep in mind that outfit boxes, instruction sheets, and even most Lionel wrapping paper are all datable. The ability to date these items is extremely useful; an outfit box dated as 1960 cannot possibly include an engine that was not issued until 1964, or contain rolling stock that dates from 1953. For purposes of dating items, as well as for general information, do not underestimate the value of original instruction sheets and the *Lionel Service Manual*. They contain a wealth of facts such as coupler type, reversing sequence, and other particulars.

It is well known that not much with Lionel was carved in granite. Lionel was first and foremost a business, and a business must show a profit to stay in business. One of the means used to monitor profits was to avoid taking charge-offs for obsolescence. Obsolete items, whether trucks, boxes, finished stock, or even paint, were used until depleted. With this in mind, Charts I and II provide a framework for dating rolling stock boxes and trucks, and help the collector to avoid making significant errors.

The Lionel Corporation, as would any other business, opted to reuse as many dies and manufacturing techniques as possible with only minor alterations. For example, SP-type cabooses made in 1969 used basically the same die as the one that was introduced in late 1947. Fortunately, there are subtle (and some not so subtle) differences that distinguish a 1947 model from a 1969 example. That was a 22-year span, and an early 1950s-era 6017 caboose has no place in a 1960s set.

Similarly, the 8½-inch 6014-series boxcars introduced in the early 1950s came in three body types; however, a 6014-series Type 1 boxcar with bar-end trucks cannot possibly be a component of a set beginning with a "19" outfit number because the 19000 series did not appear until 1962. Caution is also advised when considering the purchase of any set headed by an Alco diesel unit. Late Alcos, those introduced in 1957, have completely interchangeable chassis and cabs; the only exception is that a closed pilot cab cannot be fitted on a chassis with a front coupler without a modification to either the cab or the chassis. It is also a relatively simple procedure to switch boilers and chassis between most 200 Scout-series steam engines.

Trucks and Couplers

Lionel's business was mass producing toys and trains to be played with, not creating fine collectibles which required that exacting specifications be met in every phase of the manufacturing, assembly and packaging process. Lionel produced thirteen types of trucks and numerous coupler modifications during the postwar era. (See *Greenberg's Guide to Lionel Trains, 1945-1969, Volume I, Motive Power and Rolling Stock,* eighth edition, for a detailed discussion of the development of trucks and couplers.) Trucks and couplers varied from all metal to all plastic to combinations of metal and plastic. It was of no great concern to Lionel if an outfit contained several types of trucks, or if a component itself had a mixed combination. After all, the function of a truck was only to hold axles and wheels, and to provide motion. Nonetheless, truck and coupler data is important because it *assists* the collector in properly dating production.

Body molds and heat stamping (except for forgeries) don't lie, but trucks *can* tell a false tale: truck and coupler mechanisms are easily and often changed by some collectors, and the Lionel factory continuously used out-of-production inventory until it was depleted. Even trucks that were riveted to a plastic body mold or a metal frame can be made to look original if one has the proper tools. To further complicate the issue, hobbyists make repairs and change frames quite freely between similar pieces such as 6464 boxcars, 6014 boxcars, and SP-type cabooses; when the frame is changed, the trucks and couplers often change too. Therefore, no car's value should *ever* be predicated upon truck type alone. Condition and rarity of the body determine value; an improper truck can be replaced.

Since cost was of paramount importance to Lionel when assembling promotional sets, any corner that could be shaved was shaved: less expensive fixed coupler trucks replaced those with operating couplers, and arch bar trucks were a penny or so cheaper than AAR (Timken) trucks. By 1958, bar-end metal trucks were becoming ancient history and were never used in promotional sets after that year. Moreover, post-1962 promotional sets are seldom found with components that have operating couplers at both ends. The norm was either one fixed and one operating or two fixed couplers.

Careful planning of promotional set contents allowed Lionel to balance on-hand inventory, such as trucks. Any business would opt to use already-made components, even if slightly more expensive, rather than sustain the cost of manufacturing anew.

Promotion of Outfits

The major thrust of Lionel's overall marketing strategy was to sell outfits. It was simpler to ship and control inventory on outfits than it was on individual items, and sets generated dollar volume above and beyond single-item sales. Higher sales also meant higher commissions for the salesmen. This was not a hobby for Lionel; it was business with a capital "B." Lionel's cost structure also made it good business acumen for the retailer to order outfits, since outfits cost an average of 20 percent less than the total value of the components when priced separately, and they presented a real value to the over-the-counter customer. Very few uncatalogued pieces of rolling stock were promoted individually. (Two examples that were offered independently, however, are the 6044-1X Nestle's/McCall's boxcar and the 6651 U.S.M.C. cannon car.)

With very few exceptions, O Gauge and Super O outfits catalogued by Lionel included only track, but promotional outfits were "total packages." Nothing else needed to be purchased. Sets were often promoted based upon the number of pieces it contained, and each section of track was considered a piece! Does an 87-piece set sound impressive? (This was 1966 outfit 19567-500.) Very much so, even though most pieces were yard signs and cardboard punch-outs. In the promotion of sets, more was better even if it meant inexpensive accent pieces.

In its mid-1950s heyday, Lionel made individual items by the hundreds of thousands and packaged sets by the thousands. However, the economy softened in the late 1950s and interest in toy trains waned; some uncatalogued sets were put into the marketplace in the 1960s, with probably as few as 200 to 250 total units packaged.

Outfit Numbering

Although most uncatalogued outfits were numbered in systems completely different from Lionel's catalogued sequence, they also follow specific patterns. In 1955, Lionel began to issue uncatalogued sets with "special" rosters. The best known retailer of these sets was Sears. Lionel also initiated a new series of numbers in 1956 for its uncatalogued and promotional sets. Three- and four-digit numbers frequented the system, but the most common were five-digit numbers introduced in 1962 that began with "19". To complicate matters, both prefixes and suffixes, often with combinations of numbers and letters, abound. The numbering pattern for uncatalogued sets marketed through general retailers is shown in greater detail in the chart in the chapter on General Retailers. Numbering anomalies will be discussed in individual listings as needed.

For purely business reasons, Lionel wanted to protect full-price customers who purchased catalogued outfits under the catalogue numbering system. Unsold or returned catalogued sets were sometimes relabeled with an uncatalogued outfit number and offered to the general toy market as close-outs. For example, the catalogued 2350 New Haven EP-5 electric set 2279W or 818 from 1957 has been observed in a box that was relabeled

"X-556". Other outfits had two numbers; one number came from the Lionel sequence (catalogued or uncatalogued) while the other was the retail stock or inventory control number of the prospective retailer. These dual-numbered set boxes are quite common.

Usually the large mail-order retail establishments, such as Sears, Spiegel, J. C. Penney, and others, prefaced the sets illustrated in their catalogues with additional data that, more often than not, did *not* appear on the outfit box. For example, the rare Sears military set 49 N 9820 (as numbered in the Sears catalogue) had only "9820" on the box itself. Besides 49 N, other prefixes that were used by Sears are 79 N, 70 N, and SR (Sears Roebuck) in the later 1960s. Other examples of numbers used in this manner include Spiegel's use of R 36 J (which sometimes did appear on the set box), Ward's use of 48 T and 48 HT, and J. C. Penney's use of X 923, X 924 and X 926.

Outfit Packaging

Postwar promotional/uncatalogued sets offered by Lionel were "Ready to Run," that is, they included both track and transformer. Catalogue specialists such as Spiegel and Sears, and others that did mail-order business, insisted upon track and transformer as part of the set. They did not want to give a customer the slightest reason not to buy, or even worse, to return the set. The goal was shopping-made-easy, as many of these sets were directed toward the first-time buyer who was not familiar with electric toy trains.

Lionel's packaging was excellent and usually contained everything necessary to operate and maintain a train set right in the outfit box. These items included wire, lockon, oil, lubricant, and, when necessary, SP smoke pellets along with a wooden plunger, smoke fluid, power bus connectors, and even a battery in some years, as well as the appropriate item(s) to uncouple and/or operate the contents. Drawings for unique track plans were always included. Lionel began to include billboards with all its sets in 1950 and followed this practice into the mid-1960s.

Initially, an instruction manual was included with all but the lowest-end sets, which had their own special outfit instruction sheets. From 1955 on, the manual was reserved for top-of-the-line O27, O Gauge, and then Super O outfits while low and moderately priced O27 sets were given generic instruction sheets that depended upon the contents, i.e., type of transformer, method of uncoupling, diesel or steam, etc. In 1959, Lionel routinely started to print some specific numbered outfit instruction sheets for the low, moderate and uncatalogued O27 Gauge sets.

Other miscellaneous items included in sets were a service station directory and an accessory and/or consumer catalogue. In 1958, a sheet informing the consumer that the 1008 camtrol was attached to a piece of straight track was sometimes enclosed, and beginning in 1960, the model railroader was advised to "Lubricate Car

Axles." Warranty cards and merchandise order forms also began to appear in 1961.

Quite often the uncatalogued/promotional outfit box was of the same design and type as those used in the consumer line; at other times, Lionel utilized a nondescript generic outfit carton. Generic boxes were ordered in bulk from various suppliers and shipped flat in bundles to the Lionel factory. These boxes were usually dated in some manner when manufactured, and several common sizes were kept on hand. It is not uncommon, therefore, for a set with 1964 components to be packaged in a box dated 1963 because the box ordered and received in 1963 was not used until the following year. Generic boxes were simply rubber stamped with the appropriate outfit number at the time of packaging.

On occasion, Lionel used boxes that were totally different, as evidenced by the style used for the Halloween General set and Gifts Galore outfit X617. Outfit boxes with special graphics and logo were sometimes used by major retailers, such as Sears, Penney and Ward, during the mid-1960s. These outfit boxes were handsome and well intended, but ultimately posed another problem for Lionel. Lionel surely gave certain sales guarantees to major customers, and when sales expectations fell short, orders for unshipped trains were canceled and unsold merchandise sometimes returned. What was to be done with these sets? Returns and cancellations meant additional handling and possible repackaging expenses, especially for sets in boxes that had special graphics. Because of these problems, and additional cost factors associated with special packaging, Lionel discontinued the use of unique boxes after 1966, and reverted to using generic outfit cartons for the entire product line.

Substitutions

The problems inherent in studying uncatalogued sets and accurately listing their contents are compounded by the lack of supporting data, coupled with the scarcity of unaltered product. Many sets have been altered through the years by collectors and dealers in an attempt to upgrade their Spartan contents or simply to "fill up the box." (Additional comments on substitutions can be found under Product Authenticity.) Every time a set changes ownership, it potentially loses some credibility; each ownership change creates the opportunity for adding or removing cars and replacing broken pieces with similar but intact items.

The Lionel factory took its share of liberties with set components. Sometimes when an item intended for a particular set was prematurely depleted, Lionel replaced that item with a similar one or one of equivalent cost. Promotional sets were thus the means by which Lionel was able to deplete overstocked, unsold inventory. Occasionally, a more expensive item of higher quality surfaces in an uncatalogued set, probably for the following reason: If Lionel were left with inventory on an item at the end of the season, it was usually not carried forward at full-cost value; through an accounting function, Lionel lowered the book value of the item which, in layman's terms, means it marked down the price. The item in question then became an ideal candidate for a promotional set. Sealed outfit boxes also could hide unauthorized substitutions.

Many orders were placed by trade customers for whom wholesale cost was far more important than the roster of contents; promotion-oriented customers who were purchasing from Lionel were not nearly so concerned with what went into a set as they were with what they had to pay for it. Dollars and cents were the main factors in determining the end result—the outfit that appeared on the store shelves. Lionel often ambiguously listed set contents, for example, "33 Piece Electric Train Set" or "Five Unit Set—Locomotive, Tender, and Three Pieces of Rolling Stock." Retailers usually did not care if the tender were streamlined or slope-back, if the caboose were red, yellow or brown, or if the initially agreed-upon tank car were exchanged for a hopper. They were satisfied as long as they were not "short changed," and the wholesale cost remained constant. When accepting orders, Lionel no doubt advised promotional set buyers that it reserved the right to substitute contents based upon inventory position.

The Importance of Boxes

The importance of boxes must be stressed. A collectible item, even a tin wind-up toy, is not complete without its original box, if one exists. A collectible book with its jacket, for example, brings a premium, and the same principle applies to trains.

It is a simple fact that there are more trains than boxes in the marketplace. Not too many years ago outfit and component boxes were excess baggage. They were often one step away from the door, which meant the trash can. Many collectors shunned boxes because of storage problems, and how many of us have heard from a parent or spouse, "Get rid of those darn boxes." Many boxes have also been damaged because of improper care. Have not nearly *all* of us stored boxes in damp basements, or handled them with less than delicate, loving care?

Generally speaking, a component box adds 10 to 15 percent to the value of an item, and a crisp uncatalogued/promotional outfit box adds another 15 to 20 percent to the value of the components. These numbers are of major concern as they can increase the total value of the set by as much as 35 percent.

This has not always been the case. For example, ten years ago a complete boxed set could be purchased for roughly a 20 percent discount *below* the value of the components. Boxed sets were usually broken up and sold separately because the individual items brought more than the total package. Today a collector may expect to pay a 20 percent premium; that is a major turnaround of 40 percent!

Of course, the condition of the box should be at least equal to that of the item(s) it contains. Bear in mind that many promotional sets came with unboxed components and should be valued accordingly. There are some outfit boxes that are so scarce that they are more valuable than their common contents.

In real estate, the phrase of paramount importance is "Location, Location, Location." In the field of train collecting the words are "Condition" and "Rarity." There are no substitutes for condition or rarity in the collecting field. Even common items bring a premium when they are in Mint condition. The easiest sets to resell are top-condition pieces in clean outfit boxes. "Blue Chip" trains, just like Blue Chip stocks and bonds, are the safest investment. In addition, Like New and Mint examples of trains, as with other collectibles such as stamps or coins, will appreciate at a much faster pace than Good or Excellent items, proving themselves to be the best long-term investments.

As discussed in Collecting Uncatalogued Sets, it is essential in today's marketplace to carefully evaluate prospective purchases. Most sellers overgrade their merchandise. Unfortunately, fakes and unmarked reproductions of rare items and post-factory assembled sets are now rampant and are tainting our hobby. In addition, there exists a condition among collectors in all hobbies referred to as "the Santa Claus syndrome." Just as a child wants to believe in Santa Claus, collectors frequently cannot see the problems in their prospective purchases. The desire to own clouds the buyers' judgment and can cause collectors to view items or sets of highly questionable authenticity as legitimate, because they *want* to believe! You are urged to be a "Doubting Thomas," and keep in mind an old adage, "If it's too good to be true, it probably isn't."

Chart I

A Quick Reference Guide to Dating Trucks

1945–mid-1946:   Staple-end truck with early coil coupler (no stake marks) mounted with a pivot stud and a horseshoe clip.

Mid-1946–1947:   Same as 1945 to mid-1946, but with a late coil coupler and stake marks.

1948–1949:   Staple-end truck with a magnetic coupler without the extra hole in the activator flap.

1950–late 1951:   Same as 1948 to 1949, but with the extra hole in the activator flap.

Late 1951–1954:   Introduction of the bar-end truck with a pivot stud and magnetic coupler.

1955:   A transition year that saw the introduction of both the new bar-end truck mounted with a push clip and the extended tab coupler.

1956:   Same as 1955, but with a silver knuckle pin. *Note:* Silver pins occasionally surface on some late 1955 production, and black pins continued to surface in 1956 as on-hand inventory was depleted.

1957–1962:   Another transition period that began with the phasing out of metal trucks on O27 rolling stock, and the introduction of the early plastic AAR (Timken) truck with a metal knuckle and silver pin.

1959:   Introduction of the plastic arch bar truck that was developed for the General set, and the inexpensive advance catalogue and uncatalogued sets.

Late 1961–1962   Same as 1957 to 1962, but on some production a Delrin knuckle (without pivot points) replaced the early metal knuckle.

1962–1963:   Same as late 1961 to 1962, but with a plastic, self-contained Delrin knuckle (with pivot points) that eliminated the need for a knuckle pin. *Some* examples had an integral copper leaf spring.

Late 1963–1969:   Introduction of the open journal box late AAR truck with the axle ends visible when viewed from the bottom, and with a self-contained Delrin knuckle. The fixed coupler version of this truck appeared before the operating coupler; hence, many late 1963 and 1964 items appear with mixed trucks.

Note: The plastic leaf-spring version of the Delrin knuckle is extremely fragile and susceptible to breakage. Many pieces of Like New rolling stock surface with missing leaf springs.

For more detailed information on trucks, please refer to Chapter XII in *Greenberg's Guide to Lionel Trains, 1945-1969, Volume I*, eighth edition.

Chart II

A Quick Reference Guide to Dating Rolling Stock Boxes

1945:   Art Deco type with bold lettering. Many boxes were overstamped prewar issues.

1946:   Art Deco type with bold lettering.

1947:   Same as 1946, but with Toy Manufacturers Association logo.

1948–early 1949:   Introduction of the Early Classic box of the postwar era with smaller lettering; the stock number printed on all four sides; and the city names "NEW YORK", "CHICAGO", and "SAN FRANCISCO".

Mid-1949–1954:   Same as 1948 through early 1949, but "SAN FRANCISCO" eliminated.

1952:   Same as mid-1949 through 1954, but with OPS (Office of Price Stabilization) stamping.

1955:   Same as mid-1949 through 1954, but with some major design, size, and liner changes.

         A. Liners eliminated from all steam engines, not to reappear until the reissue of the 773 Hudson in 1964.

         B. Liners eliminated from all tenders.

         C. Liners eliminated from all F-3 power and tender units.

         D. Liners eliminated from all 2500-series passenger cars.

         E. Redesigned smaller single-piece cardboard insert for the 6419 work caboose and for new-issue 6119-series work cabooses.

         F. Wraparound liner eliminated from diesel switchers in favor of two small cardboard filler pieces.

         G. Redesigned, less complex single-piece cardboard insert for 6560 cranes.

1956–1958:   Same as 1955, but the stock number was eliminated from the four sides.

1958:   Same as 1956-1958, but *some* with bolder-faced type on the end flaps.

1959–1960:   Solid orange with tear-out perforated front.

1961–1964:   Orange and white with picture of a steam and F-3 locomotive on the front, and the city names "NEW YORK" and "CHICAGO". Earliest issues were a distinctly darker orange.

1965:   Same as 1961-1964, but "HILLSIDE" replaced "NEW YORK" and "CHICAGO" and with the new corporate name, "THE LIONEL TOY CORPORATION".

1966:   Cellophane see-through front with a rubber-stamped stock number.

1967:   No production.

1968:   Lionel checkerboard pattern with "HAGERSTOWN" on the end flaps, usually with a rubber-stamped stock number.

1969:   Same as 1968, but with "HILLSIDE" on the end flaps.

Note: Most promotional sets came without component boxes. Like other items, boxes were used until depleted. It is not uncommon to find a box dated to a specific year appearing one or two years *after* it was discontinued.

Chart III

Nomenclature for Postwar Paper-type Boxes

A. Art Deco:	The original postwar component box with bold blue lettering that touched the tops and bottoms of the blue frames and outlines.
B. Early Classic:	The most notable box of the postwar era introduced in 1948 for the O27 line with smaller lettering; the city names "NEW YORK", "CHICAGO", and "SAN FRANCISCO"; and with the stock number printed on all four sides.
C. Middle Classic:	Same as Early Classic, except the city name of "SAN FRANCISCO" was eliminated. It was used from mid-1949 through 1955.
D. OPS Classic:	Same as Middle Classic, but with the inclusion of the OPS stamp. It was used in 1952.
E. Late Classic:	Same as Middle Classic, except that the stock number was eliminated from the four sides. It was used from 1956 through 1958.
F. Bold Classic:	Same as Late Classic, but with a much bolder-faced print on the end flaps. It was used for part of the 1958 product line.
G. Glossy Classic:	A scarce box that surfaced in 1958. It was made in the Classic design, but was printed on coated stock similar to what was introduced in 1959. The 3424 Wabash brakeman, for example, occasionally came in this type of box.
H. Orange Perforated:	A dramatic change in graphics that was a total departure from the classic design. The box was orange coated stock that had a tear-out perforated front panel. It was used in 1959 and 1960.
I. Perforated Picture:	This box occasionally surfaced in 1961 and 1962. It was not regularly used, but was simply a means by which to deplete unfinished, perforated-front "raw" stock. It sometimes appears with a rolling stock item, but its use was most prevalent for early issue Presidential passenger cars.
J. Orange Picture:	A variation of the Orange Perforated without perforations and with a picture of a steam and F-3 locomotive on the front, and the city names "NEW YORK" and "CHICAGO". It was used from 1961 to 1964 and included the phrase "THE LIONEL CORPORATION".
K. Hillside Orange Picture:	Similar to Orange Picture, but "HILLSIDE" replaces "NEW YORK" and "CHICAGO". It was used for part of the 1965 product line and included the new corporate name, "The Lionel Toy Corporation".
L. Cellophane Front:	This was Lionel's attempt to make package contents visible by adding a cellophane window to the front of the box. The stock number was no longer printed on the end flaps as part of the manufacturing process; it was now rubber stamped and was used in 1966.
M. Hagerstown Checkerboard:	Another dramatic change in graphics. This 1968 box had a Lionel checkerboard pattern with "HAGERSTOWN" printed at the bottom of the end flaps. Because their use was restricted to a single item, the 6560 crane and 260 bumper, for example, had a type-stamped stock number while other multiple-use boxes had the stock number rubber stamped.
N. Hillside Checkerboard:	Same as Hagerstown Checkerboard, except that "HILLSIDE" replaced "HAGERSTOWN" in 1969.
O. Last Resort:	When everything else was depleted, Lionel sometimes reverted to using a plain generic white or "Last Resort" box during the late 1960s. Most were rubber stamped, but an occasional type-stamped example does surface.

Chart IV

A Quick Reference Guide to Dating O Gauge Outfit Boxes

1945:   Conventional tan with paste-on label.

1946:   Same as 1945

1947:   Same as 1945.

1948:   Same as 1945.

1949:   Conventional tan with orange and blue printing directly on the box.

1950:   Conventional tan with an orange field framed in blue with blue printing and most with the retail price.

1951:   Conventional tan with blue frame (no orange field) and blue printing, and most with OPS price stamping.

1952:   Same as 1951.

1953:   Conventional tan with red frame, blue printing, a large circled-L, and the retail price.

1954:   Same as 1953.

1955:   Same as 1953, but without the retail price and the phrase "1955 Outfit" either within or outside of the blue frame on box end.

1956:   A dramatic change—the introduction of the tan-gray basket weave design.

1957:   Same as 1956.

1958–1963:   No catalogued production. Several sets have been reported from 1958-1959 with O Gauge track. These sets were probably assembled to lessen the factory position on over-stocked inventory. Even though sets were not catalogued, O Gauge track was continuously offered in the catalogues for separate sale during these years.

1964:   Conventional nondescript tan with black rubber-stamped set number, and the early release of the white 1965-style box.

1965:   Conventional type, solid white with orange lettering, except catalogued outfit 12800 which was packed in a Type D display-style box. These were generic boxes that included a rubber-stamped outfit number.

1966:   Same as 1965.

1967–1969:   No production.

Chart V

A Quick Reference Guide to Dating O27 Gauge Outfit Boxes

O27 and O Gauge outfit boxes were the same for all years 1946 through 1957. This chart does *not* include uniquely designed set cartons or those with special graphics for specific retailers. Be advised that by 1961 most outfit boxes regardless of type were no longer preprinted with the set number. Instead, the boxes were generic and rubber stamped at the time of packaging.

1958: Tan-gray basket weave design that originated in 1956.

1959: Introduction of the attached perforated-lid Type A, B, and C display boxes on a yellow background for the low and moderate outfits. Better outfits were packaged in a conventional-type box (also on a yellow background) while the advance catalogue and some uncatalogued sets came in a unique Type A display-style box on a white background. Other uncatalogued sets came in a conventional generic tan outfit carton.

1960: A combination year that included some outfits with Type A, B, and C yellow background display-style boxes the same as in 1959, and others with new half-orange, half-white graphics that included a sketch of a 4-6-2 Pacific steam engine on the upper portion of the lid.

1961: Low and moderate outfits came in boxes the same as in 1960 with the half-orange, half-white graphics in Type A or B only, while the better sets were packaged in a conventional solid orange box. The advance catalogue sets and some uncatalogued sets came in a Type A display-style box on a white background with deep red print and graphics that were later adopted for the 1963 consumer line.

1962: Same as 1961.

1963: Low and moderate outfits (both catalogued and uncatalogued) in a Type A display-style box with *new* orange and white graphics. The box lid pictured a small Hudson-type steam engine and a Santa Fe F-3. The better sets and some uncatalogued sets were packaged in conventional tan set cartons.

1964: The same artwork on the display-style box as in 1963, but now the top was completely unattached and lifted off. This is referred to as the Type D display-style box. Some uncatalogued sets came in the newly recolored O Gauge box which was a conventional type on a white background with orange lettering.

1965: Type D display-style box (both catalogued and uncatalogued) with Hillside logo and new graphics. A 2037 steam engine pulling a string of freight cars was now pictured on a white background. Some uncatalogued sets also came in the white background conventional box introduced late in 1964.

1966: Same as 1965.

1967: No catalogued production.

1968: Type D display-style box with special Hagerstown graphics for catalogued outfit 11600. Uncatalogued outfits were packaged in a conventional tan box, or carryover 1965 Type D display-style boxes.

1969: Conventional two-tier box on white background with red and blue printing and a picture of the outfit pasted on one end for catalogued sets. Uncatalogued sets often came in carryover 1965 Type D display-style boxes, or more routinely in conventional tan outfit cartons.

Description Key for display-type boxes:

Type A — Perforated attached top with interior channels or cardboard dividers.

Type B — Perforated attached top with one-piece die-cut interior filler.

Type C — Perforated attached top with no interior channels but with component boxes.

Type D — Lift-off top with interior channels.

Note: Occasionally a nondescript tan conventional outfit box surfaces in years in which it should not. One can assume that this may have been a special packing request by a customer, such as a company that did mail-order business, or that the limited numbers packed did not warrant the special ordering or reordering of a regular outfit box.

COLLECTING UNCATALOGUED SETS

Catalogued or Uncatalogued?

The purpose of this book is to provide a comprehensive listing, with contents and current values, of uncatalogued Lionel sets, and to identify by cross reference outfit numbers in which contents were identical to that of catalogued sets. For example, Sperry and Hutchinson's (S & H) set 6P-4810 was identical to Lionel's catalogued set 11331, and is listed in the chapter on General Retailers as "11331/6P-4810". Furthermore, as explained in the Prologue, Lionel sometimes labeled their catalogued outfits with an uncatalogued number to purposely mislead the buying public and to "lose" the outfits in the marketplace. We also believe that all of the late 1940s to mid-1950s Sears outfits were identical to Lionel's consumer catalogue line, except for the Sears inventory control/retail stock number, and we have identified these sets by *both* numbers in a chart contained in the Sears chapter. Packaging for uncatalogued sets often differed from the Lionel consumer line. This book will point out those differences. Lionel catalogued approximately 420 sets, give or take a repeat number or two, during the postwar era, and it is believed that as many (if not more) uncatalogued sets were available during that period. We have been able to positively identify about 260 uncatalogued outfit numbers for this book.

Within the context of this book, an *uncatalogued* set is defined as any set or outfit that either did not appear or was not offered in Lionel's advance catalogue or consumer catalogue. The term *advance catalogue* refers to the catalogues that were sent to dealers and distributors of Lionel trains, while the *consumer catalogue* indicates catalogues that were widely available to the public. *Promotional* sets are those that were assembled to promote the name and/or product of a manufacturer or retailer. For example, Gifts Galore set X617 promoted the company name by means of a special outfit box, whereas outfit X-589 promoted RCA Whirlpool by displaying its name on a special-issue boxcar. A promotional set can also mean one considered by the general buying public to be

an exceptional value; many were assembled by Lionel and offered to retailers simply to promote (sell) overstocked inventory or to keep their factory running. The companion volume, *Greenberg's Guide to Lionel Trains, 1945-1969, Volume III, Sets*, provides carefully documented data on regular production catalogued sets and the promotion-oriented advance catalogued outfits; readers are encouraged to refer to that volume for additional information.

Promotional sets were usually made to sell at the low end of the spectrum to entice buyers. However, not every uncatalogued set was oriented toward promotion. Several were produced to sell at even premium prices. For example, Sears 2347 C & O Geep outfit 9836 shown in their 1965 catalogue had a retail price of $99.95; only 1965 Lionel consumer catalogued set 12780 and the impressive Hudson Super O outfit 13150 were priced higher. Sets similar in content and price to Lionel catalogued offerings were often sold by various retailers to capitalize on the well-known Lionel trade name. For simplicity, and because these are the terms collectors use, the words *uncatalogued* and *promotional* are used interchangeably in this text. Lionel used the words *outfit* and *set* interchangeably during the postwar period, as we do here.

Determining Values

Outfit values in this book have been determined by both *estimated* and *obtained* prices. We do not have adequate sales history to determine market value accurately on many of the less notable sets listed.

Toy train values vary for a number of reasons. First, consider the *relative knowledge* of the buyer and seller. A seller may be unaware that he has a rare variation and sell it for the price of a common piece. Another source of price variation is *short-term fluctuation* which depends on what is being offered at a given train meet on a given day. A related source of variation is the *season* of the year. The train market generally is slower in the summer and sellers may then be more inclined to reduce prices if they really want to move an item. Another important source of price variation is the relative strength of the seller's *desire to sell* and the buyer's *eagerness to buy*. Clearly a seller in economic distress will be more eager to strike a bargain. A final source of variation is the *personalities* of the seller and buyer. Some sellers like to turn over items quickly and, therefore, price their items to move; others seek a higher price and will bring an item to meet after meet until they find a willing buyer. Hobby shops are also an important vehicle for the buying and selling of trains.

Another factor which may affect prices is reconditioning done by the dealer. Some dealers take great pains to clean and service their pieces or sets so that they look their best and operate properly. Others sell the items just as they have received them, dust and all. Naturally, the more effort the dealer expends in preparing his items for sale, the more he can attempt to charge for them. This factor may account for significant price differences among dealers selling the same equipment.

Many Like New items have been uncovered under a layer of dust. Keep in mind that dust, in most instances, can be removed while rust and dents cannot. Sellers often tend to "over-clean" their merchandise. Keep a watchful eye for items that have been given a coat of wax or oil, and for those that have had their wheels cleaned. Wheel cleaning is usually accomplished by using a wire brush attachment on a motor tool or by the use of gun blue applied with a cotton swab. This practice may be acceptable to some for Very Good items but it is not acceptable for a Like New grade. Be aware of anything that is the color silver, and note that most red-painted and red heat-stamped items are extremely sensitive to dust and cleaning.

From our studies of train prices, it appears that mail-order prices for postwar Lionel trains and outfits are generally higher than those obtained at train meets. This is appropriate considering the costs and efforts of producing and distributing a price list, and packing and shipping items. Mail-order items may sell at prices above those listed in this book.

We receive many inquiries as to whether or not a particular item or outfit is a "good value." This book will help answer that question; but, there is *no substitute* for experience in the marketplace. *We strongly recommend that novices do not make major purchases without the assistance of friends who have experience in buying and selling trains.* If you are buying a set and do not know whom to ask about its value, look for the people running the meet or show and discuss with them your need for assistance. Usually they can refer you to an experienced collector who may be willing to examine the outfit and offer his opinion. Keep in mind that many sellers have a no-return policy.

Since many trains have been produced in a wide variety of colors, it is important to view a potential purchase under bright, incandescent lights or outdoors. Occasionally, collectors will confuse colors in show facilities and basements due to the low levels of light in these locations or the shifted color spectrum caused by fluorescent lights. For example, it is not unusual to mistake dark blue for black in a dully lit room.

Pricing Criteria

Many factors were considered in determining set values. First and foremost was the box data. A set that came from the factory with component boxes is of greater value than the same or a comparable set that was shipped without component boxes. The scarcity of the outfit box itself and the rarity (i.e., collectibility) of the items it contained were also taken into account. For example, the 1882 Halloween General set box alone commands a price in excess of $1000 in today's market while other boxes with common nondescript engines and rolling stock have minimal value. Outfits with unique track plans and accessories stir collector interest far more than those with a simple, run-of-the-mill oval. Outfits that contained a 1033 transformer or one with a whistle/horn controller such as 1053 bring a slight premium over those shipped with a 1012 or 1015. Also considered was the type of track included in the set. A circle of Super O, along with several straight pieces and a No. 37 uncoupling section, generally adds about $50 to the value of the set.

If you have trains to sell and you sell them to a person planning to resell them, you will not obtain the prices reported in this book. Rather, you should expect to achieve between 50 and 70 percent of these prices for ordinary items. For highly desirable items in Like New condition, a higher percentage of the price is often obtained because the demand exceeds the supply. Basically, for your items to be of interest to a buyer who plans to resell them, he must purchase them for considerably less than the prices listed here.

Condition

For each outfit, we provide two price categories: **VERY GOOD** and **LIKE NEW**. Collectors, however, are reminded that there are other categories commonly used as well, and we have included them here for reference. As a guide, the following definitions may be used to determine an item's condition.

FAIR — Well-scratched, chipped, dented, rusted, or warped.

GOOD — Scratches, small dents, dirty.

VERY GOOD — Few scratches, exceptionally clean, no major dents or rust. *Must include* the outfit box and component boxes where applicable, with allowance for normal wear. It is always preferable, though not mandatory, to have box liners and associated paperwork along with miscellaneous items such as lubricant and smoke pellets. O27 and O Gauge track are optional because they have minimal resale value in Very Good condition, but Super O track should be included along with the related uncoupling/operating items. Although desirable, low-end transformers are not mandatory; better transformers, such as those with a whistle/horn control, are of importance because of their greater resale value.

EXCELLENT — Minute scratches or nicks, no dents or rust, all original with less than average wear. The other criteria are the same as those mentioned under the VERY GOOD description.

LIKE NEW — Only the faintest signs of handling and wheel wear with crisp, vibrant colors that show no evidence of polishing. The outfit box and component boxes where applicable must be in comparable condition with no major rips or tears. A Like New box must have all the end flaps, ears, and coupler protection flaps attached. Like New condition *must* include all box liners, instruction sheets, miscellaneous items, and the appropriate track and/or transformer. Super O track and related items, and transformers with whistle/horn controllers have substantial resale value.

MINT — Brand new, absolutely unmarred, all original and unused, with the outfit box, and component boxes where applicable, and with any additional items that came with the set, such as instruction sheets, factory inspection slips, billboards, track, manuals, etc. There is often substantial confusion in the minds (or perhaps simply difference of opinion) of both sellers and buyers as to what constitutes "Mint" condition. How do we define Mint? Among very experienced train enthusiasts, Mint means that it is brand new, never run, and extremely bright and clean with crisp original component box(es). An item may have been removed from the box and replaced in it but it should show no evidence of display or use. Long-term shelf display of Mint items will usually lessen their value; a piece is not Mint if it is dust covered, scratched or discolored, even though it was never run. It is not uncommon, however, for an absolutely brand-new item to show telltale signs of handling and even to have some touch-up paint. These instances often occurred at the factory, where many a dirty, greasy hand picked up an item and left finger marks for eternity on what would otherwise be absolutely perfect merchandise. Because many items were also stacked during production and shelved without boxes prior to shipping, scratches were inevitable.

RESTORED — Professionally refinished with a color that approximates the original finish. Trim and ornamentation are present and in Like New condition. The finish usually appears in at least Like New condition.

REPRODUCTION — A product intended to closely resemble the original item. Although the Trains Collectors Association (TCA) requires that it should be marked as a reproduction in order to be sold at a TCA-sponsored meet, often it is not. Reproductions and reproduction parts are currently available for many desirable items, and more than a fair share of diesel and electric engines have been upgraded with reproduction decals: buyers are urged to exercise extreme caution.

The decision to purchase or not to purchase always rests with the buyer. Some buyers' criteria are more stringent than others. Collectors sometimes frown upon the inclusion of track in outfits because track is quite apt to cause damage to the far more valuable boxes or scratch unboxed items.

In the toy train field there is a great deal of concern with exterior appearance and less concern with operation. If operation is important to you, then ask the seller whether the train runs. If the seller indicates that he does not know whether the equipment operates, assume that it does not, and we recommend that it should be tested. Most train meets have test tracks provided for that purpose. (For items in Mint condition it is *not* recommended that you even test run the equipment.)

It is the nature of a market for the seller to see his wares in a very positive light and to seek to obtain a higher grade price for a lower grade item. In contrast, a buyer will see the same item in a less favorable light and will attempt to buy a higher grade set for the price of one in lower grade condition. It is our responsibility to point out this difference in perspective *and* the difference in value implicit in each perspective, and to then let the buyer and seller settle or negotiate their different points of view.

Sets which are determined to be truly Mint in condition—by both the buyer and seller—will bring a substantial premium above the prices shown for Like New. Again, we strongly recommend that novices exercise extreme caution, since restored, fraudulent, and reproduction items are all quite prevalent in the marketplace.

Sources of Information

Seeking advice is especially important because of the ever-present danger posed by fakes and frauds. Unethical persons have chemically altered common pieces to change either the color of the body or lettering and have offered them as rare variations. We urge our readers to exercise extreme caution when purchasing Lionel postwar outfits with equipment purported to be a "factory error" or preproduction because of a difference in color or graphics. The Factory Prototypes and Errors chapter in *Greenberg's Guide to Lionel Trains, 1945-1969, Volume II, Behind the Scenes* (second edition) contains entries which are known to be genuine factory errors. Readers should consult expert opinion before contemplating any such purchase.

The Lionel collector and operator has several additional sources for toy train information. The selection of Greenberg publications available for your library includes Guides to prewar, postwar, and modern era trains; operating and repair manuals; catalogues; and an upcoming encyclopedia with expanded information on postwar items. In addition to many Lionel references, we also publish books on many other major and minor train and toy manufacturers.

Reporting Postwar Variations

The main reason for the success of Greenberg's Guides has been the response and interest of you, the collector and enthusiast. Over the years collectors from all over the United States and Canada have written with comments, suggestions, and advice. These contacts have enabled the Guides to become more accurate and thorough. We are very pleased with the eagerness with which readers have responded, and hope that they will continue to do so with our uncatalogued sets Guide.

The decision-making process concerning proposed new listings or revisions is surprisingly complex—and sometimes quite agonizing. Sometimes the inclusion of a set component is difficult to establish, and follow-up letters asking for specific information reveal that the component does not date to the purported year. At other times a really odd item or set roster may strain one's credulity, yet the listing is genuine. Our criteria will be most stringent. In general, there are three major criteria used by the authors before listing a new entry, or before amending an existing one:

(1) CREDIBILITY: We are trying to answer the classic question of the skeptic: "How do you know this outfit came as such from the factory?" The difficulties in determining credibility are presented by the following example. We have two independent reports on outfit 19434, but each report contains an entirely different list of contents! One set has predominately military-related olive drab items and is headed by a very scarce 221 Santa Fe Alco A unit; the other contains run-of-the-mill rolling stock but includes a 216 M St. L ALco A unit. Which set is correct? In this instance, because of grossly conflicting data, we cannot list either one. *Our goal is to have three independent reports for each outfit that we list.*

(2) CORROBORATION: Many times the type of proof sent along with the report is crucial. Photographic evidence is an absolute *must*. Of equal importance is independent verification by other knowledgeable collectors. Again, our goal is to have three independent reports for each outfit that we list.

(3) COMPLETENESS: The more complete your description the better. We want all the information you can give in describing the engine and rolling stock, but we are also most interested in packaging and in the miscellaneous items that came with the outfit, such as track, transformer and instruction sheets. Again, our criteria will be most stringent. We *will not* list any set unless it is accompanied by an outfit box; the box is our first source of information because it gives us the outfit number.

If you wish to report a new entry or correction to us, please use the reporting sheet enclosed with this book. We appreciate very much your cooperation, enthusiasm and good will in helping us document Lionel uncatalogued train set production. As has been our custom, we will acknowledge any comments noted in this Guide as your observation. Every letter to us will be answered.

Important References

In writing this book, the authors assume that the reader has a basic understanding of and familiarity with postwar Lionel trains. Whether a novice or an experienced collector, *Greenberg's Guide to Lionel Trains, 1945-1969, Volumes I, II* and *III* are most valuable companions when reading this work as they give excellent information on Lionel trains, sets and associated items.

Volume I, Motive Power and Rolling Stock is the classic reference to *regular production* postwar motive power and rolling stock. It does not include errors and prototypes. Errors and prototypes are listed in a detailed chapter in *Volume II, Behind the Scenes*. Both Volumes contain references to sets that will be of interest to readers of this guide. *Volume III* comprehensively lists every postwar advance and consumer catalogued set. It also furnishes the hobbyist with sections on component boxes and outfit box descriptions, along with complete appendices of every postwar set and catalogued engine, and an explanation of outfit numbering during the mystery years 1955, 1956 and 1957.

The Listings

This Guide is organized by the sequential listing of verified uncatalogued outfit numbers, *not* by individual years or engine numbers. Separate chapters are devoted to sets sold by major retailers—Sears, Montgomery Ward, Spiegel, J. C. Penney, and Firestone. Promotional sets sold by other businesses are listed in the chapter on General Retailers. Each listing begins with the outfit number and year of issue. Some outfit numbers include NA and NAA suffixes, but unfortunately, we are unable to explain their meaning. A slash ("/") between numbers in the *heading* means that either *both* numbers appear somewhere on the outfit box, or that the outfit is identifiable by either number. Unless otherwise noted, the number on the left indicates the retailer's stock number while the number on the right identifies Lionel's uncatalogued number. For example, Spiegel set 5260/19507 shows Spiegel's 5260 and Lionel's 19507. A slash ("/") in the *comments* portion of the listing indicates that the outfit can be identified by the number on either side of the slash, or that the lettering on either side of the slash appears on different lines of the item. Unless specifically stated otherwise, it is presumed that the outfit was an O27 Gauge set. A list of the set contents is followed by a discussion of the set, and Very Good and Like New values conclude each listing. *The values stated require an original outfit box.*

An overview of the gauges and track used by Lionel during the postwar period will help the reader put uncatalogued sets in perspective. All of the trains (except HO) that Lionel produced during the postwar period operated on three-rail track with a measurement of 1¼ inches between the running rails. This track is commonly known as *O Gauge*. Track was produced, however, in three varieties: O27, O, and Super O. Each of these types of track has its own unique characteristics and is not readily interchangeable. *O27 Gauge* was made of a lightweight metal with a height of 7/16 inches, and eight curved track sections form a circle with a diameter of 27 inches. *O Gauge* track was made of heavier metal with a height of 11/16 inches, and eight curved track sections form a 31-inch circle. *Super O* was a specialized track system introduced by Lionel in 1957 and consisted of realistic plastic ties with T-shaped running rails. The center rail was replaced by a thin copper blade that allowed electrical contact. Twelve sections of curved Super O track form a circle with a diameter of 38 inches. All O27 items could be run on O Gauge track, and most on Super O, but the converse is not true. Larger O Gauge items such as the 773 Hudson and 2500-series passenger cars have difficulty negotiating the "tight" curves of O27 track; they also interfere with O27 switch motors.

Sets assembled during this period contained only one type of track, not a mixture. Most O27 sets were less expensive than either O Gauge or Super O, but the top-of-the-line O27 outfits were often substantially more expensive than the introductory O and Super O sets. However, Super O was considered to be Lionel's premium merchandise. Because most uncatalogued/promotional sets were O27 Gauge, they were usually priced towards the medium and low end of the scale. There were, in contrast, some notable exceptions, which are discussed in the text.

The reader will notice that considerable attention has been given to outfit boxes and component boxes where applicable. To the serious collector, authentic boxes are essential to the credentials of an outfit, and an outfit is not really complete without the appropriate boxes.

The contents of outfits are listed as Lionel listed them—by their catalogue stock number, which sometimes included a suffix, by the number that appears on the proper component box, or by the *Lionel Service Manual*

listing. In many cases the *Service Manual* listings are the only means by which to identify an item. Some items were lettered but not numbered while others were neither numbered nor lettered; the numbers for those items appear in parentheses. For example, the olive drab rescue unit caboose that is lettered both "LIONEL" and "RESCUE UNIT" is unnumbered. It was never listed by number in any catalogue, but it is listed in the *Service Manual* as "6119-125", and appears in this book as "(6119-125)". To cite other examples, we specifically state that the yellow work caboose that appears as "(6120)" in this book is unstamped, meaning that it was neither numbered nor lettered. The 6167 SP-type caboose, however, has two separate listings; it is listed as "6167" when the number 6167 is present on the car, but is also listed as "(6167)" when referring to other 6167 cabooses that are unstamped. Suffixes such as "-60" and "-85" that appeared on some boxes from the 1957-1959 era are for the most part insignificant, while other suffixes such as "-100" and "-125" from the mid-1960s often denoted load or coupler type.

The tenders included with most of the steam engines pose an additional problem. Even though we are able to identify most of them by number through our own research, tenders usually do *not* include a stamped Lionel stock number. However, be aware that most of the early postwar tenders (through about 1956) had a Lionel stock number rubber stamped on the underframe. For this volume, parentheses appear only with tenders that are completely unstamped examples, i.e., those on which wording such as "LIONEL LINES" and "SOUTHERN PACIFIC" is *not* present. The *Pocket Guide to Lionel Catalogued Sets* contains an abbreviated article on tenders that you will find most informative.

Since much of this book examines Lionel trains in an original way, it has been necessary to coin new terms in order to categorize this material clearly. Readers will find the Glossary and the nomenclature chart in the Prologue helpful in understanding these terms.

Sears, Roebuck and Co.

THE GOLIATH FROM CHICAGO

Although Lionel flirted with other catalogue retailers, such as Montgomery Ward, Spiegel and J. C. Penney during the postwar era, Sears was their steady date. Like any relationship, business or otherwise, theirs was tumultuous at times, but it was indeed deep and long lasting. Lionel postwar products appeared in Sears catalogues continuously from 1946 through 1967. At this time we have been unable to verify any catalogue listings for 1968 and 1969, but we state with confidence that Lionel products were sold over-the-counter at selected Sears stores during those two years.

During the postwar era, Sears was the nation's leading retailer. They were also Lionel's largest dollar volume customer. Chicago was their base of operation, just as it was for their competitors, Montgomery Ward and Spiegel. Chicago, in essence, was (and still is) the transportation center of the United States. In addition to a network of major highways, it has access to water routes via Lake Michigan, and is also a major airline and railroad hub. What better place for a company that was a giant in the mail order business to choose as national headquarters?

The major portion of business for most retailers is done in the fourth quarter. That statement applies to both over-the-counter and mail-order specialists, and Sears was both. Toy trains were definitely a gift, or fourth-quarter item; hence, their major exposure was in the Sears Christmas catalogue. Sales through the Christmas catalogues far exceeded the sales generated by spring, summer, fall, and regional catalogues combined.

Because of the diversity of their business, Sears employed both corporate and regional buyers (purchasing agents) in addition to a catalogue buying staff. The corporate toy buyer placed orders for items (toy trains probably included) that would have national exposure over-the-counter at most Sears retail stores, while regional buyers, usually working out of the regional office, would place orders for items pertinent to a region, i.e., beachwear for Florida and heavy outerwear for Maine. Lionel salesmen undoubtedly called upon regional buyers in order to place additional Lionel product within the region at Sears stores and/or in regional catalogues. That is probably why Sears train sets sometimes are found for which we cannot locate a catalogue listing. On the other hand, the catalogue buyers were probably a separate group, working with national buying authority out of the Chicago office.

Assembling a catalogue as massive as the Sears Christmas issue was a difficult, to say the least, and thankless project. Decisions had to be made many months in advance. Beside sets, numerous separate-sale items were featured in Sears catalogues, including track, transformers and accessories. Lionel probably had staff assigned to work exclusively with Sears catalogue personnel. Production had to be scheduled, packaging determined, shipping coordinated and sales monitored. That was not a job for the fainthearted. During Lionel's glory years, the easiest task was to sell the goods; headaches came from every other facet of the business.

A chart has been included in this chapter that lists all Sears outfits that we can currently identify, catalogued and otherwise, in numerical sequence. We have deleted all prefixes and suffixes that appeared with the catalogue listing and list only the four-digit Sears stock number; that was usually the *only* number printed on the set carton. Occasionally, a Sears outfit surfaces with a small Sears price sticker marked with both the retail price and an inventory control number. From our observations, it seems that some of these sets may never have been featured in a nationally issued catalogue, and may have been sold solely over-the-counter at a Sears store. For instance, we cannot locate any catalogue listing for 1958 outfit 9659. An example of this set has been reported in a basket weave outfit carton that was numbered "9659" by Lionel, but the carton also showed a miniature price sticker marked "8A 49 9659" and "$59.95". (Note the absence of any letter following "49".) Another example of a Sears outfit reported with a price sticker is set 9672. This set was featured in a 1961 national-issue Sears Christmas catalogue as outfit 49 N 9672 at $29.88. However, the example reported to the authors came in a generic tan outfit carton that was Lionel factory stamped with only the number "9672", while the sticker read "1A 49 9672" and had the retail price marked at $29.99. From this information, we conclude that some Sears outfits were available both as feature items in a catalogue and over-the-counter purchases.

The Sears catalogue prefaced Lionel listings with 49 or 79, followed by a letter; for example, "49 N 9668" and "79 T 9651". The numbers 49 and 79 were used randomly for both outfit and separate item prefixes. However, most sets were prefaced with "79" while most separate-sale items utilized "49". These numbers were also used interchangeably between lower and higher priced items, and items with lighter and heavier shipping weights. The letter that followed the 49 or 79 prefix varied depending upon season, region, or year of catalogue issue. The practice of using a letter as a code for catalogue identification is still common among mail-order retailers in today's market. For example, the letter "N" was consistently used for items and outfits featured nationally in the Sears Christmas catalogue every year, while letters such as D, E, G, K, T, and U were utilized in various fall issues, and possibly in regional catalogues. Each catalogue used only one letter throughout its listings. Some outfit listings also included a suffix such as C, K, L, and T. For example, 1959 outfit 79 N 9682K was a Super O set while 1965 set 79 N 9836K was an O Gauge outfit. Perhaps the K designated a major accessory; the 1959 outfit included a rocket launcher while the 1965 set included a manual culvert unloader. Other outfits that were catalogued with a C or L suffix also included accessories, while the T suffix, used from 1946 to 1954, is not significant.

Another problem encountered when analyzing the Sears numbering system is that Sears often reused an outfit number. For example, numbers 9653 and 9655 were used three times! A collector must be familiar with outfit boxes if he is to determine which Sears set 9653 is in question; outfit boxes are easily datable by graphics and logo (refer to Charts IV and V, included with the Prologue).

Another numbering variable arose in 1964. Beginning in that year *some* Sears outfit boxes were marked with both the four-digit Sears number and a five-digit Lionel number from the uncatalogued "19" series. For example, the set carton for 1964 Sears outfit 9813 was also marked at the factory with the Lionel number 19325, but another 1964 Sears set, military outfit 9820, was identified only by the number 9820. Some 9800-series outfit boxes also had the set number prefixed by "SR" (Sears Roebuck). In the late 1960s Lionel outfits, numbered only in the five-digit uncatalogued "19" series, and probably not exclusive to Sears, were retailed over-the-counter at certain Sears stores.

Sears packaging was identical to Lionel packaging through 1958 and outfit box descriptions were the same as those explained in Charts IV and V. In 1959 "different" boxes began to appear; many Sears outfits, even Super O sets, were packaged in generic tan set cartons. We have never observed any Sears outfit in a display-style set box; all Sears outfits came in conventional set cartons. We assume this was done to facilitate shipping and handling; if used in shipping, display-style boxes were cumbersome and would not have adequately protected the contents. Furthermore, we can state with near certainty that all 9800-series Sears outfits, which first appeared in 1964, were packaged in unique set cartons with Allstate graphics. (There are two variations of Allstate set cartons; later issues illustrate more artwork.) Several of these boxes are pictured in this chapter.

Component boxes for engines and rolling stock are seldom found with any Sears outfit that post-dates 1962. Set contents were usually separated and held in place by cardboard dividers. However, as a rule of thumb, accessories such as the 346 manual culvert unloader came in component boxes.

The manner in which Sears advertised and packaged Lionel sets is confusing, to say the least. We suggest that you reread the introduction after a good night's sleep and a hearty breakfast. As you read the listings in this chapter, you will note that only one prior to 1955 is given. That is because *all* Sears outfits shown in their catalogues before 1955 were identical to Lionel outfits, were packaged in the same manner, and were retailed at the same price as Lionel suggested in their own consumer catalogue. For discussion and contents of these catalogued outfits, we suggest that you refer to the companion book, *Volume III*. During 1955 circumstances changed with the onset of discount retailing. The 1955, 1956 and 1957 Lionel consumer catalogues no longer listed suggested retail prices and outfit numbers because discounting had become the business norm. Outfits with contents different from Lionel catalogued sets began to surface. The first such Sears outfit was the 1955 Burlington Geep set, Sears number 9652, that most often (or perhaps always) was packaged in a conventional Lionel outfit carton that was uniquely numbered as "505X". At the same time, Sears began to price their outfits on an average 15 percent less than comparable or, in some instances, identical Lionel catalogued sets.

Through our research, we have uncovered some pricing disparities in various Sears catalogues on identical Lionel outfits after 1954. For example, 1955 outfit 9651 was featured by Sears in their fall catalogue as set 79 T 9651 with a price of $25.95, while the same set was also illustrated in the 1955 Sears Christmas catalogue as outfit 79 N 9651, priced at $26.45. We also have noticed price differences in Christmas catalogues (with N in the outfit number) for different regions of the country in the same year. For example, one catalogue that originated from the Chicago area had 1957 outfit 79 N 9641 priced at $29.43, while the 1957 Sears Christmas catalogue for the East Coast had the same outfit, also listed as 79 N 9641, but priced at $29.95. These minor discrepancies are commonplace and no doubt relate to shipping costs. Such differences in pricing make sense when the postal factor is taken into account; freight charges for shipments routed from Chicago to the far west, south and eastward had to exceed those for shipments made within the Midwest region. UPS, for example, currently has the continental United States divided into six rate zones.

Much of our analysis was done through catalogue research, and Sears catalogues have been our major source of information. Unless specific mention of a report or ownership is made at the end of a listing, it should be assumed by the reader the Sears catalogue was our sole source of information.

Sears Outfits

Sears Outfit Number	Comparable Lionel Catalogued Number	Engine(s)	Gauge	Year(s) Catalogued by Sears
5939	1461S	6110	O27	1950
†5940	1112	1001, 1101	O27	1948
†5940	1117	1110	O27	1949
††5946	1405W	1666	O27	1947
5950	1463W	2036	O27	1950
5951	1463WS	2026	O27	1951
5954	1423W	1655	O27	1948, 1949
5955	1469WS	2035	O27	1950, 1951
5958	1467W	2023	O27	1950, 1951
5960	1431	1654	O27	1947
5961	1431W	1654	O27	1947
5966	1435WS	2025	O27	1947
†††5967	1427WS	2026	O27	1948
†††5967	1451WS	2026	O27	1949
5970	1453WS	2026	O27	1949
5976	1403	221	O27	1946
5977	1403W	221	O27	1946
5980	2125WS	671	O	1947
5981	2137WS	675	O	1948
5982	2147WS	675	O	1949
5985	2173WS	681	O	1950, 1951
5987	2105WS	671	O	1946
9601	1001	610	O27	1955
9602	none	626	O27	1956
9603	1000W	2016	O27	1955, 1956
9606	none	2016	O27	1956
9613	1553W	2338	O27	1956
9640	none	250	O27	1957
9641	none	611	O27	1957
9642	none	2037	O27	1957
9643	none	2339	O27	1957
9651	1465	2034	O27	1952
9651	1527	1615	O27	1955
9652	505X	2328	O27	1955
9652	none	225	O27	1960
9653	1477S	2026	O27	1952
9653	1533WS	2055	O27	1955
9653	none	243	O27	1960
9654	1485WS	2025	O27	1952
9654	none	226	O27	1960
9655	1479WS	2056	O27	1952
9655	none	248	O27	1958
9655	none	2365	O27	1962
9656	1467W	2032	O27	1952, 1953
9656	none	210	O27	1958
9656	none	218	O27	1962
9657	none	2037	O27	1958
9657	none	2037	O27	1962
9658	none	2337	O27	1958

Sears Outfit Number	Comparable Lionel Catalogued Number	Engine	Gauge	Year(s) Catalogued by Sears
9658	none	736	Super O	1962?
9659	1513S	2037	O27	1954
9659	none	665?	unknown	1958?
9661	1500	1130	O27	1953
9661	none	unknown	unknown	1959?
9662	1501S	2026	O27	1953
9664	1503WS	2055	O27	1953, 1954
9664	none	unknown	O27	1959
9665	1505WS	2046	O27	1953
9665	none	2348	O27	1959
9666	none	1862	O27	1959
9668	1543	627	O27	1956, 1957
9670	1523	6250	O27	1954
9670	none	246	O27	1961
9671	1517W	2245	O27	1954
9672	none	233	O27	1961
9673	2187WS	671	O	1952
9673	none	218	O27	1961
9675	none	736?	Super O?	1961?
9682	2211WS	681	O	1953
9682	none	44	Super O	1959
9683	2217WS	682	O	1954
9683	none	unknown	unknown	1959?
9687	2225WS	736	O	1954
9692	none	2037	Super O	1960?
9693	none	218	Super O	1960
9694	none	746	Super O	1961?
9723	unknown	1062	O27	1967
9724	19733	635	O27	1967
9730	unknown	218	O27	1963
9732	19706	215	O27	1967?
9807	unknown	237	O27	1964
9808	19557	1062	O27	1966
9810	19561	635	O27	1966?
9813	19325	1061	O27	1964
9820	unknown	240	O27	1964
9834	unknown	237	O27	1965
9835	19454	216	O27	1965
9836	12885?	2347	O	1965

Notes:

† In 1949, Sears relisted their 1948 outfit 5940. We do not know if this was the same as 1948 Lionel set 1112 or the comparable 1949 Lionel set which was catalogued by Lionel as outfit 1117.

†† Outfit 1405W was catalogued by Lionel in 1946, but it was not featured in the 1947 Lionel consumer catalogue. However, the 1947 Sears catalogue featured set 5946 which was identical to the 1946 Lionel roster. We do not know if the Sears set was leftover 1946 Lionel production of outfit 1405W which included a 1666 engine with number plates and a 1041 transformer, or 1947 Lionel advance catalogue set 3105W which included a rubber-stamped 1666 and a 1042 transformer. If Sears catalogue sales of their set 5946 were strong, Lionel may have serviced their needs with both outfits.

††† Sears used their number 5967 in both 1948 and 1949, but the Sears catalogue clearly illustrated a different Lionel set for each year.

Question marks (?) after the date in the Year(s) Catalogued by Sears column indicates that the authors cannot locate a catalogue listing for the outfit. However, we have included a date based on outfit box description and/or our analysis of Sears outfit numbers. Other question marks also indicate a lack of confirmation.

5940 / 1112   1948

Contents: 1101 die-cast steam locomotive; 1001T Scout sheet metal tender; 1002 blue Scout gondola; 1004 Baby Ruth Scout boxcar; 1005 Sunoco Scout tank car; 1007 red Scout SP-type caboose; 8 curved, 3 straight, 1009, 1011 transformer.

Comments: Although this set is nothing more than Lionel catalogued outfit 1112, its contents are worthy of a special note. Reviewing the 1948 Lionel catalogue leads one to believe that both this outfit and the companion Scout set 1111 were headed by the plastic-boilered 1001. This was not the case, as outfit 1112 usually (maybe always) contained a die-cast engine.

A special feature about the engine that came with this particular set is that it was erroneously rubber-stamped "1001", the Lionel number that designated the plastic engine! Lionel eventually corrected the mistake, and shortly thereafter began to rubber stamp the die-cast locomotives with the correct 1101 number. M. Nicholas Collection.

	VG	LN
With plastic 1001	75	175
With die-cast 1001	150	250
With die-cast 1101	100	200

Lionel introduced the Scout series in 1948 in order to reach customers who were willing to spend only a minimal amount. Scout couplers made integration with other regular production rolling stock, i.e., items with knuckle couplers, impossible. Lionel catalogued this outfit as 1112 while Sears offered the same set as 5940. The Lionel catalogue stated that engine 1001 (which had a plastic boiler) was included with this outfit, but examples of this set are known to contain a die-cast 1101. The set pictured above has a die-cast engine, but it was erroneously stamped "1001". Note the original engine box in the left center portion of the photograph; it has been overstamped with "1101", the correct designation for a die-cast engine. M. Nicholas Collection.

VG   LN   VG   LN

9602   1956

Contents: 626 B & O center cab; 6112 black gondola with canisters; 6014 Baby Ruth boxcar; 6560 red cab crane; 6119-25 orange DL & W work caboose; 12 curved, 3 straight, 6029, 90° crossing, 1015 transformer.

Comments This outfit was packaged in the regular 1956-issue basket weave set box. Except for the orange work caboose, the other rolling stock items are inconsequential. However, the scarce B & O center cab is very collectible. Although a new item for 1956, according to the *Lionel Service Manual* listing, the 626 was not featured in the Lionel catalogue until 1957, and was never offered in a catalogued set. J. Algozzini and P. Ambrose observation.   **450   950**

9606   1956

Contents: 2016 steam locomotive; 6026W square whistle tender; 3484-25 operating Santa Fe boxcar; 6562-25 red gondola with canisters; 6464-350 MKT boxcar; 6025 black Gulf tank car; 6257-50 SP-type caboose; 8 curved, 3 straight, 6029, 1033 transformer.

Comments: This outfit happens to be one of the best Sears sets from the mid-1950s. It was packaged along with component boxes for each item in a two-tier basket weave set carton. Unfortunately, the 2016 engine is insufficiently appreciated among many collectors because it lacks smoke and Magnetraction. Nonetheless, it is a relatively scarce engine. The two "finds" included with this outfit are the operating Santa Fe boxcar on a Type 2B body mold and packaged in a Late Classic box, and the -350 MKT (Katy) boxcar. The Katy boxcar was catalogued by Lionel for separate sale only; this is the only instance in which it is known to have been included as an outfit component. W. Corsello Collection.   **550   1000**

9640   1957

Contents: 250 red-striped steam locomotive; 250T red-striped Pennsylvania streamlined tender; (6111) flatcar with logs; (6121) flatcar with pipes; 6112 gondola with canisters; 6017 SP-type caboose; 8 curved, 2 straight, 1008 control, 1015 transformer.

Comments: Although presented as a Sears exclusive, this set does not contain any item not available in the 1957 Lionel consumer catalogue. The 250 engine was introduced in 1957 and was the first issue in the new 200 Scout series.   **125   250**

9641   1957

Contents: 611 Jersey Central diesel switcher; 6464-425 New Haven boxcar; 6262 flatcar with wheels; 6646 stock car; 6112 gondola with canisters; (6121) flatcar

with pipes; 6014/6024 8½" boxcar; 6017 SP-type caboose; 8 curved, 3 straight, 6029, 1015 transformer.

Comments: Aside from this exclusive Sears outfit, the 611 Jersey Central also headed Lionel catalogued seven-car freight set 1581/732. The rolling stock roster in the Sears outfit is almost totally different from the Lionel catalogued issue. Most (possibly all) items were component boxed and came in a common basket weave outfit carton. The 8½" boxcar was not clearly illustrated in the Sears catalogue; it could be either a 6014-series Bosco or Frisco, or even a 6024 Shredded Wheat. E. Chornyei Collection.   **425   850**

9642   1957

Contents: 2037 steam locomotive; 6026W square whistle tender; 6112 gondola with canisters; 6014/6024 8½" boxcar; (6111) flatcar with logs; 6025 Gulf tank car; 6560 red cab crane; 6119-75 gray DL & W work caboose; 8 curved, 5 straight, 6029, 1053 transformer.

Comments: 2037 steam freight sets are not high on anyone's list of outfit collectibles, especially with uninteresting rolling stock. The 2037 locomotive headed seventeen Lionel catalogued outfits, as well as fronting sets for Sears and Montgomery Ward along with other uncatalogued "specials." At least this outfit offered some play value; canisters, pipes, a crane car, and a whistle tender were usually enough to keep most youngsters amused.   **175   350**

9643   1957

Contents: 2339 Wabash Geep; 3650 extension searchlight car; 6424 flatcar with autos; 6511 flatcar with pipes; 6482 refrigerator car; 6646 stock car; 6436 Lehigh Valley quad hopper; 6467 miscellaneous car; 6119-25 orange DL & W work caboose; 8 curved, 7 straight, 6029, 1044 transformer.

Comments: This outfit was a Sears exclusive and was described in their catalogue as "Huge 9 Unit Diesel Freight with remote-control horn". All items were component boxed and came packaged in a two-tier basket weave set carton. Although this outfit contained O27 Gauge track, the 2339 was catalogued by Lionel as an O Gauge engine and headed catalogued O Gauge outfit 2275W/815. The 6646 stock car and the 6482 reefer are under-appreciated rolling stock items; they were catalogued by Lionel for only one year and were components of only one catalogued set. E. Dougherty Collection.   **600   1200**

9652 / 505X (multiple use of number)   1955

Contents: 2328 Burlington Geep; 6465 Sunoco tank car; 6456-25 gray Lehigh Valley hopper; 3484-25

The engine and rolling stock included with 1960 outfit 9652 were regular production Lionel items, but they were assembled in a roster exclusive to Sears. Number 9652 had previously been used by Sears in 1955, but can easily be distinguished from the earlier issue by the outfit box; remember that outfit boxes can be dated, and this example had graphics completely different from the 1955 issue. Notice the Bold Classic 6119-100 caboose box; it was a carryover from 1958. This outfit contains a rare collectible variation, namely the 6817 earth scraper with wire windshield. P. Michael Collection.

	VG	LN

operating Santa Fe boxcar; 6257 SP-type caboose; 8 curved, 3 straight, 6019, 1033 transformer.

Comments: This outfit appears to be the first Sears catalogue offering that did *not* duplicate the Lionel catalogue set. The 1955 Lionel catalogue offered the Burlington Geep in freight outfit 1531W/505 that also included a hopper and tank car, but the third rolling stock item was a 6462 gondola, not the operating boxcar as listed with the Sears set. We assume a change was made because the identical Lionel catalogued set was featured in the 1955 Montgomery Ward catalogue.

To differentiate this outfit, the Sears set carton was stamped "505X". (505 was Lionel's three-digit number that corresponded to 1531W.) We assume the "X" was added because of the rolling stock change and to avoid potential shipping errors. The illustration in the 1955 Sears catalogue pictured an operating boxcar with the Pennsylvania Road name, but this set usually contains a 3484-25 Santa Fe. W. Banovitz Collection.   **450   1000**

9652 (multiple use of number)   **1960**

Contents: 225 C & O Alco A unit; 6361 timber transport; 6817 flatcar with earth scraper; 6812 track maintenance car; 6670 flatcar with boom crane; 6119-100 red/gray DL & W work caboose; 8 curved, 1 straight, 6029, 1015 transformer.

Comments: This outfit was packaged with individually boxed components in a generic tan two-tier set carton. Even though this was a 1960 outfit, the work caboose still came in a 1958 Bold Classic box. An exceptionally rare variation of the 6817 earth scraper was a usual component of this set; it was an example with a wire windshield. The 6670 flatcar with boom crane (sans out-

1958 Sears outfit 9656 closely resembles Lionel catalogued set 1599, which was also headed by the 210 Texas Special Alco units. The 6465 tank car and the 6424 flatcar with autos were replaced in the Sears issue by the 6802 flatcar with girder and the black 6476 hopper. 1958 was a transition year, and this outfit contained a mixture of Late and Bold Classic boxes. The 9656 number was previously used by Sears in 1952 and reused for the third time in 1962. A. Tolli Collection.

	VG	LN

rigger supports) is a scarce rolling stock item. P. Michael Collection. **700 1400**

9653 (multiple use of number) **1960**

Contents: 243 steam locomotive; 243W square whistle tender; 6062 gondola with cable reels; 6014-100 Airex boxcar; 6825 flatcar with trestle bridge; 6017 SP-type caboose; 8 curved, 3 straight, 6029, 1063 transformer

Comments: The 243 engine was new for 1960, and even though it was a plastic-boilered Scout engine, it was equipped with a liquid smoke unit and was paired with a whistle tender. This Sears outfit also included the un-catalogued red -100 Airex boxcar. All contents were component boxed and were packaged in a generic tan single-tier outfit carton. T. Randazzo Collection.

150 325

	VG	LN

9654 (multiple use of number) **1960**

Contents: 226P/226C Boston & Maine Alco AB units; 6470 exploding boxcar; 3830 flatcar with operating submarine; 6650 flatcar with IRBM launcher; 3419 flatcar with operating helicopter; 6017 SP-type caboose; 8 curved, 5 straight, 6029, 1063 transformer.

Comments: This exclusive Sears outfit was headed by the uncatalogued Boston & Maine Alco units, and that fact alone makes it collectible. The rolling stock roster was an impressive array of military-related items, but the caboose appears to be a disappointment. Instead of a complementary blue 6017-100 Boston & Maine caboose, the caboose illustrated in the Sears catalogue was an inconsequential 6017 Lionel Lines. We assume that all items were component boxed. As a point of information, Mint boxed examples of the 226 AB units were available over-the-counter at Madison Hardware well into the mid-1980s. **400 850**

	VG	LN

9655 (multiple use of number)   **1958**

Contents: 248 steam locomotive; 1130T streamlined tender; 6014 Bosco boxcar; 6112 gondola with canisters; 6476 Lehigh Valley hopper; 6151 flatcar with Range Patrol truck; 6017 SP-type caboose; 8 curved, 2 straight, 1008 camtrol, 1015 transformer.

Comments: This outfit came with component boxes in a conventional two-tier basket weave set carton. The rolling stock items were common from the 1958 Lionel product line, but the 248 was a new engine. It was not catalogued by Lionel and was the first uncatalogued issue in the 200 Scout series. Uncatalogued outfit X-610 NAA was also headed by the 248 engine. T. Randazzo Collection.   **175   400**

9655 (multiple use of number)   **1962**

Contents: 2365 C & O Geep; (3349) turbo missile launcher; 6463 rocket fuel tank car; 6448 exploding box-

car; 6413 Mercury capsule carrying car; 6017 SP-type caboose; 8 curved, 1 straight, 6029, 1010 transformer.

Comments: This exclusive Sears military set was about as good as any set featured in the Lionel catalogue. The 2365 C & O Geep also headed one Lionel catalogued outfit; it is often confused with the much rarer 2347 C & O Geep with horn, that headed 1965 Sears outfit 9836. The Lionel catalogued set also featured four rolling stock items (three premium cars and a duplicate of the 3349) and was priced in their catalogue at $49.95, while the Sears issue was sold through mail order at a surprisingly low $29.75. The Sears outfit box, like the Lionel, was a solid orange conventional two-tier type that included component boxes for each item. M. Sokol Collection.   **500   1100**

9656 (multiple use of number)   **1958**

Contents: 210P/210T Texas Special Alco AA units; 6801 flatcar with boat; 6014 orange Bosco boxcar; 6112

As shown above, Sears outfit 9657 is dated to 1958; the same number was used again by Sears in 1962. All contents were regular production items. Note the mixture of Late and Bold Classic boxes, the norm for 1958, and the presence and absence of suffixes. The -60, -85 and -135 suffixes from 1957-1958 have continued to confuse collectors; the use of a specific suffix was not limited to a particular set. Furthermore, different colors of rolling stock, such as with 6112, 6014 and 6476, were never consistently relegated to a specific box. The authors do not know why "N 619" was written on the outfit box. E. Reising Collection.

VG   LN

blue gondola with canisters; 6802 flatcar with girders; 6476 black Lehigh Valley hopper; 6017 SP-type caboose; 8 curved, 3 straight, 6029, 1015 transformer.

Comments: For many years this set was believed to be the same as Lionel catalogued outfit 1599. The assumption was that collectors substituted some rolling stock items; they did not! Inspection of an original unaltered set reveals that the Lionel factory amended the contents so that it would differ from the catalogue issue. The 6465 Sunoco tank car and the 6424 flatcar with autos from outfit 1599 were replaced in the Sears set with the 6802 and 6476. The Sears outfit carton was a conventional two-tier basket weave style (as was Lionel set 1599), and all items were component boxed. A. Tolli Collection.

250   500

9656 (multiple use of number)   **1962**

Contents: 218P/218C Santa Fe Alco AB units; 3419 flatcar with operating helicopter; 3665 Minuteman boxcar; 6448 exploding boxcar; (3349) turbo missile launcher; 6017 SP-type caboose; 8 curved, 3 straight, 6029, 147 horn controller, 1073 transformer.

Comments: This was the third Santa Fe Alco set to grace the Sears catalogue. This set again paired an Alco B unit with a powered A unit, but unlike 1961 Sears outfit 9673, this set had an entire roster of military-related rolling stock. It was loaded with action as every car "did something." Unfortunately, the military items were very fragile and did not hold up well in the hands of playful children.

Though we have not been able to examine an outfit first hand, we assume, because of companion 1962 Sears sets 9655 and 9657, that the set carton was a solid orange conventional two-tier type, and that all items were component boxed. Sears priced this outfit at $39.77 while a comparable space-related set headed by a 229P/229C M St. L Alco pair had a suggested retail price of $49.95 in the Lionel consumer catalogue.   325   700

9657 (multiple use of number)   **1958**

Contents: 2037 steam locomotive; 6026W square whistle tender; 6476 black Lehigh Valley hopper; 6800 flatcar with airplane; 6014 red Bosco boxcar; 6112 black gondola with canisters; 6818 flatcar with transformer; 6017 SP-type caboose; 8 curved, 5 straight, 6029, 1044 transformer.

Comments: There is nothing spectacular about this outfit. All items were component boxed and came in a two-tier basket weave outfit carton. The rolling stock was all routine issue from the 1958 Lionel product line, and a 6818 without broken insulators is becoming difficult to find. The best item in the set is the 6800 flatcar with yellow over black airplane. An unbroken, Like New example will usually bring more money on the resell market than the combination of a 2037 engine with a whistle tender. E. Reising Collection.   275   525

VG   LN

9657 (multiple use of number)   **1962**

Contents: 2037 steam locomotive; 233W or 234W square whistle tender; 3370 sheriff and outlaw car; 6445 Fort Knox car; 3376 operating giraffe car; 6473 rodeo car; 6361 timber transport; 6017 SP-type caboose; 8 curved, 3 straight, 6029, 1063 transformer.

Comments: This was the only steam freight set featured in the 1962 Sears Christmas catalogue. Though none of the items are difficult to obtain, this was an action-packed, visually appealing set that included five colorful rolling stock items. With a Sears catalogue price of $49.77, it was one of the higher ticket Lionel train sets to be featured in the 1960s.

All items were component boxed and came in a solid orange conventional two-tier set carton. The 1962 Lionel catalogue also featured a traditional 2037 steam freight set, and it was priced comparably at $49.95. However, the rolling stock roster offered with the Sears set was far superior to the that which was shown in the Lionel catalogue. V. Bibelot Collection.   325   650

9658 (multiple use of number)   **1958**

Contents: 2337 Wabash Geep; 6800 flatcar with airplane; 6464-425 New Haven boxcar; 6264 flatcar with lumber load; 6818 flatcar with transformer; 6424 flatcar with autos; 3361 operating log car; 6560 red cab crane; 6119-100 red/gray DL & W work caboose; 8 curved, 7 straight, 6029, 1044 transformer.

Comments: This was the second consecutive year that Sears catalogued a nine-unit Wabash Geep set, but this outfit roster was completely different from the 1957 issue. The 2337 was a new Wabash number for 1958; it was fitted with non-operating couplers, hence the number change from 2339. The outfit carton was a two-tier basket weave style, and all items were component boxed in a mixture of Late and Bold Classic styles. W. Pike Collection.   600   1200

9658 (multiple use of number)   **1962**

Comments: We have been unable to locate any Sears catalogue listing for this outfit. It has been reported as a 736 Super O freight set, packaged in a solid orange conventional two-tier outfit carton. J. Algozzini observation.

9659 (multiple use of number)   **1958**

Comments: At present, we have not found any Sears catalogue listing for this set. It reused an outfit number that was previously assigned in 1954 to what was then the equivalent of catalogued Lionel outfit 1513S.

This outfit is usually mistaken for the 1882 Halloween General set, but it actually differs in nearly every respect. 1959 Sears outfit 9666 came in a generic tan outfit box, and was headed by the 1862 General and included a simple oval of track. Note the assembled Plasticville 963 Frontier set; the contents were the same as what was included with the Halloween General, but the component box was different. The box for 963 (top left) was a Glossy Classic design and did not include a -100 suffix. See comparison photograph of box 963 and 963-100 on page 120. J. Algozzini Collection.

	VG	LN

This outfit box was a conventional two-tier basket weave type with a "58" date on the underside of the set carton and included a Sears price sticker marked "$59.95". We do not know the contents, but the set was purportedly headed by a 665 steam engine. D. LeGore observation.

9661 (multiple use of number)　　　　**1959**

Comments: Unfortunately, we can report nothing about this outfit except for the existence of a set carton. It was a generic tan conventional two-tier type that reused a set number previously assigned in 1953 and 1954. We date this outfit to 1959, based upon the set box description and the Sears chronology of outfit numbers. P. Ambrose observation.

9664 (multiple use of number)　　　　**1959**

Contents: 200 Scout-series steam locomotive and tender; 6162 gondola with canisters; 6014 Bosco boxcar; 6825 flatcar with trestle; 6017 SP-type caboose; 8 curved,

1 straight, 6029, 1053 transformer.

Comments: This outfit was illustrated in the 1959 Sears Christmas catalogue. The engine shown in the catalogue was the blue-striped 247 B & O, but we believe this to be an error because the caption states "smoke and whistle". The 247T was *not* a whistle tender. The engine may have been a 2018, 245, or possibly a 243 that was not catalogued by Lionel until 1960.　　**75**　**150**

Note: Values are questionable because engine has not been identified.

9665 (multiple use of number)　　　　**1959**

Contents: 2348 M St. L Geep; 3419 flatcar with operating helicopter; 6572 Railway Express reefer; 6818 flatcar with transformer; 6062 gondola with cable reels; 6476 Lehigh Valley hopper; 6017 SP-type caboose; 8 curved, 3 straight, 6029, 1053 transformer.

Comments: This particular set exemplifies how Lionel "blended" old and new products. The 2348 was catalogued in 1958 by Lionel to head a Super O outfit; by 1959 it was surplus inventory, as were the carryover 6572

	VG	LN

and 6818. They were offered to Sears in an O27 Gauge set along with a hopper car and a caboose, and two new 1959 items, the 3419 and 6062. Although we have not been able to examine a set first-hand, we assume that all items were component boxed. **550 1000**

9666 1959

Contents: 1862 General steam locomotive; 1862T General tender; 1865 passenger car; 1866 mail/baggage car; 1877 flatcar with horses; 963 Plasticville Frontier set; 8 curved, 2 straight, 1015 transformer.

Comments: This is the set that is usually mistaken for the 1882 Halloween General outfit. We will bury that myth forever, because the outfits differ in almost every respect. This outfit came packaged in a tan generic two-tier set carton and included component boxes for each item. By comparison, the Halloween General was shipped in a unique flat pack with die-cut filler (refer to the chapter on General Retailers, page 121, for more information). The only items common to both sets are the 1866 mail/baggage car and the Plasticville Frontier set, but the example of the 963 included with the Sears set came in a Glossy Classic box while the graphics on the 963-100 box from the Halloween General were unique. J. Algozzini Collection. **450 900**

9670 (multiple use of number) 1961

Contents: 246 steam locomotive; 244T slope-back tender; 6476 Lehigh Valley hopper; 6162 gondola with canisters; 6050 Lionel savings bank car; 6825 flatcar with trestle; 6017 SP-type caboose; 8 curved, 1 straight, 6029, 1010 transformer.

Comments: The inconsequential contents of this outfit could bore one to tears. All components were regular production Lionel catalogue items. The Sears catalogue price was $18.88, which to this date was the least amount ever charged for a Lionel train set in any Sears publication. **100 200**

9672 1961

Contents: 233 steam locomotive; 233W square whistle tender; 6825 flatcar with trestle; 6162 gondola with canisters; 6465-110 Cities Service tank car; 6017 SP-type caboose; 8 curved, 3 straight, 6029, 1063 transformer.

Comments: This 1961 Sears outfit was a slightly better offering than the companion steam freight set 9670. At least the plastic-boilered 233 engine was equipped with a liquid smoke unit and was paired with a whistle tender. The 6825 appears as a rolling stock item in an inordinate number of Sears outfits from the era. All items were component boxed and were packaged in a generic tan conventional two-tier set carton. D. Jackson Collection. **150 250**

9673 (multiple use of number) 1961

Contents: 218P/218C Santa Fe Alco AB units; 3665 Minuteman boxcar; 3419 flatcar with operating helicopter; 6476 Lehigh Valley hopper; 6162 gondola with canisters; 6017 SP-type caboose; 8 curved, 5 straight, 6029, 1063 transformer.

Comments: This was the second consecutive year in which a Santa Fe Alco set was featured in the Sears catalogue. This edition, however, paired an Alco B unit with the powered A unit, and was downgraded from Super O to an O27 Gauge set. The rolling stock roster was ill conceived; conventional freight items and military cars do not relate well. The 1961 Lionel catalogue also featured the Santa Fe Alco in an AB pair with a more traditional consist of items. The Sears outfit came packaged, just as did the Lionel set, in a solid orange conventional two-tier set carton with component boxes. K. Rubright Collection. **300 600**

9675 1961

Contents: 736 Berkshire steam locomotive; 736W streamlined whistle tender; 6530 fire inspection car; 6428 U.S. Mail car; 6463 rocket fuel tank car; 6736 Detroit & Mackinac quad hopper; 6357 SP-type caboose; 12 curved, 3 straight, 1 insulated straight, 39-25 operating packet, 1063 transformer.

Comments: As opposed to the more typical O27 Gauge outfits sold through Sears, this was a Super O set! We have been unable to locate a catalogue listing for this set; quite possibly it was featured regionally, or may have been sold over the counter through a small group of Sears retail outlets. No matter where it was sold, the set was about as impressive as any outfit featured in the 1961 Lionel catalogue. All items were component boxed and were packaged in a conventional, solid orange two-tier set carton. D. Julio Collection. **350 700**

9682 (multiple use of number) 1959

Contents: 44 U.S. Army mobile missile launcher; 6650 flatcar with IRBM launcher; 6470 exploding boxcar; 6175 flatcar with rocket; 6807 flatcar with military DKW; 6814 medical caboose; 175 rocket launcher; 12 curved, 1 straight, 1 insulated straight, 39-25 operating packet, 1053 transformer.

Comments: This is assuredly one of the best Lionel outfits that was offered in the Sears catalogue during the postwar era. Most Sears sets were O27 Gauge, but this was a Super O outfit. All military items are in collector demand, especially if intact and unbroken, and this set was military, all the way. The 175 rocket launcher, a poor-selling, fragile accessory, was also a component of Channel Master set 9745 and 1959 catalogued outfit 2545WS. **700 1500**

At first glance, 1960 Sears outfit 9692 appears to be nothing more than a common steam freight set. The 2037 engine was the Lionel standard-bearer of the O27 Gauge steamers. It headed seventeen catalogued sets and numerous uncatalogued issues. Although not unheard of, outfit 9692 included Super O track! Observe that the outfit box was generic rather than the standard Super O style. In only one outfit (2555W) did Lionel include a transformer with a catalogued Super O set. Note that outfit 9692 included a 1063 transformer, a prerequisite for retailers who did mail-order business. J. White Collection.

VG LN

9683 (multiple use of number) **1959**

Comments: At this time, we can give no information about this set, except for a description of the outfit box. It was a tan generic two-tier type that used an outfit number that had been previously assigned in 1954. Sears outfit 9682 was issued in 1959 with Super O track, and because of the 9683 number of this set, we assume that this was a Super O outfit. A. Vincent observation.

9692 **1960**

Contents: 2037 steam locomotive; 243W square whistle tender; 6361 timber transport; 6825 flatcar with trestle; 6062 gondola with cable reels; 6821 flatcar with crates; 6017 SP-type caboose; 12 curved, 1 straight, 1 insulated straight, 39-25 operating packet, 1063 transformer.

Comments: The roster of contents included with this outfit would lead one to believe that it was just another routine O27 Gauge steam freight set, but that

would be a wrong assumption. This exclusive 1960 Sears outfit was assembled with Super O track. At present, we cannot locate a catalogue listing; it may have been featured in a regional catalogue or sold over-the-counter at a Sears retail outlet. The set carton was a generic tan conventional two-tier type, and all items were component boxed. J. White Collection. **275 500**

9693 **1960**

Contents: 218P/218T Santa Fe Alco AA units; 3419 flatcar with operating helicopter; 6816 flatcar with bulldozer; 3444 animated gondola; 3512 fireman and ladder car; 6017 SP-type caboose; 12 curved, 1 straight, 1 insulated straight, 39-25 operating packet, 1063 transformer.

Comments: This exclusive Sears outfit is one truly worth owning. Even though the 218 Santa Fe Alco pair was catalogued by Lionel as O27 Gauge, it was offered in the 1960 Sears catalogue with Super O track. All items were component boxed and were packaged in a conventional, solid orange two-tier outfit carton. The rolling stock was exceptionally noteworthy, with the 3512 and 6816 being very much in collector demand. This set has also been reported to contain a 6017-185 gray ATSF caboose in lieu of the 6017 Lionel Lines. P. Adler observation.   **600   1300**

9694   1961

Contents: 746 Norfolk and Western steam locomotive; 746W Norfolk and Western streamlined whistle tender; 3419 flatcar with operating helicopter; 3330 flatcar with submarine kit; 6544 missile firing trail car; 3540 radar scanning car; 3535 security caboose; 12 curved, 3 straight, 1 insulated straight, 39-25 operating packet, 1063 transformer.

Comments: We can only speculate as to why the mighty Norfolk and Western appeared at the head of a Sears outfit. The 746 was first catalogued by Lionel in 1957, and it headed a total of five Lionel sets catalogued through 1959. We assume that Lionel grossly overestimated its sales projection for this engine. Component boxes for the engine and tender, along with manufacturing

techniques and the original instruction sheet, date production to 1957, yet in 1961 Lionel was still staring at unsold inventory. The Norfolk and Western was offered for separate sale in the Lionel catalogue and to Sears with a roster of military cars. Lionel also appeared to have produced too few tenders in the initial run, and subsequently was forced to scramble and produce some additional tender inventory; hence the rubber-stamped, long-striped variation of the 746W tender.

This outfit was packaged in a solid orange conventional two-tier set carton, and all items were component boxed. We cannot locate a Sears catalogue listing for this outfit; it may have been featured in a regional catalogue, or because of the undoubtedly high retail price, sold over-the-counter at a Sears store located in an affluent area. This outfit is illustrated in *Volume II*, first edition, page 20.   **1800   3600**

9723   1967

Comments: 1062 (2-4-2) steam locomotive; 1061T slope-back tender; 6076 Lehigh Valley hopper; (6042) unstamped gondola with cable reels; (6402) gray General-

This outfit with the uncatalogued 19733 Lionel number was available (probably not exclusively) through Sears. It was illustrated on page 523 of the 1967 Sears Christmas catalogue. Observe the full-sized red 6825 flatcar. Because of the number, one would expect it to have included a trestle bridge, but Lionel "cleaned house" in anticipation of the move to Hagerstown, Maryland, and packaged this flatcar, which dates to the early 1960s, with two cable reels instead. M. Toth Collection.

VG   LN

type flatcar with logs; (6167) unstamped SP-type caboose; 8 curved, 2 straight, 1025 transformer.

Comments: The 1967 Sears Christmas catalogue touted this as an exclusive Sears outfit. We assume that the set carton was generic and was numbered in the Lionel "19" uncatalogued series. The contents of this set were nothing to write home about, but note that the unstamped General-type flatcar carried an unusual load of three logs. The catalogue description even states "Flatcar transports husky load of timber." By 1967, Lionel put any load that was available on a flatcar.

We have an interesting piece of literature on Sears letterhead pertaining to this set. It reads, "Through an error, the locomotive in the outfit, 49N9723, $18.44, was not equipped with a headlight as shown in the catalog illustration. We are reducing the price $1.00 and trust you are satisfied with this merchandise."   75   150

9724 / 19733   1967

Contents: 635 Union Pacific diesel switcher; 6050 Swift boxcar; 6076 gray Lehigh Valley hopper; (6402-50)/6825 flatcar with cable reels; 6130 Santa Fe work caboose; 8 curved, 2 straight, 1008 camtrol, 1025 transformer.

Comments: This outfit was illustrated on page 523 of the Chicago edition of the 1967 Sears Christmas catalogue, as set 49 N 9724, at $22.66. However, the example that generated our listing was purchased through a Sears outlet store in the Chicago area. The generic tan two-tier outfit carton in which it came was stamped only with the Lionel uncatalogued number 19733.

The purchaser (M. Toth) had the opportunity to order several of these sets, and did so. All other outfits contained a red Lehigh Valley hopper, while this example contained one in gray. Note that the 6825 flatcar included with this outfit carried a load of two cable reels instead of a trestle bridge. Even the Sears catalogue illustration depicted a full-sized 6800-series flatcar with brakewheel! We assume that Lionel had "old" shelf inventory on the 6825 flatcar without a load and buried it in this set with two cable reels. Furthermore, there is a single page Sears insert within the outfit carton that makes buyers aware that the automatic uncoupler section mentioned in the catalogue is not included with this set; Lionel had temporarily run out of stock. The insert went on to say that a manual uncoupler was included with the set and that the price would be reduced by $2.50. M. Toth Collection.   200   425

9730   1963

Contents: 218P/218T Santa Fe Alco AA units; (6469) liquefied gas car; 6465 orange Lionel Lines tank car; 6464-900 NYC boxcar; 6464-725 New Haven boxcar; 6473 rodeo car; 6476 Lehigh Valley hopper; 6257-100 SP-type caboose; 8 curved, 5 straight, 6029, 1073 transformer.

VG   LN

Comments: This 1963 outfit was better than any O27 Gauge offering in the Lionel consumer catalogue. At a price of under $30, it was an exceptional value, considering that military-related Santa Fe Alco set 11385 was priced at $49.95 in the Lionel catalogue. Aside from the scarce 6469 liquefied gas car, this outfit also contained two 6464-series boxcars.   450   900

9807   1964

Contents: 237 steam locomotive; 242T streamlined tender; 6176 Lehigh Valley hopper; 6822 night crew searchlight car; 346 manual culvert unloader with 6342 culvert pipe gondola; 6059 M St. L SP-type caboose; 321 trestle bridge; 958 Plasticville vehicle set; 14 curved, 11 straight, 6149, pair of manual switches, 1025 transformer.

Comments: Most all 1964 Lionel catalogued sets were stale and unimaginative, but this outfit and companion 1964 set 9820 are Sears classics. This outfit came packaged in an elongated, oversized set carton with Allstate graphics. It included the reissue of the culvert unloader and, contrary to catalogue hype, contained not a remote-controlled but the manually operated 346. The 346 always came packaged in a corrugated accessory carton. However, early editions of the manual culvert unloader came without the culvert pipe gondola within the accessory box. The 6342 came either unboxed or in a relabeled Orange Picture box. Sears offered plenty of track with this set, 26 pieces total, along with a pair of manual switches. The 958 vehicle set, which was packaged in a plain white box with appropriate Lionel stampings, is one of the rarest of the Lionel Plasticville-series items. P. Michael, A. Stewart and M. Visnick Collections.   375   750

9808 / 19557   1966

Contents: 1062 steam locomotive; 1062T slopeback tender; 6176 black Lehigh Valley hopper; 6142 green gondola with canisters; 6059 red M St. L SP-type caboose; pair of manual switches; Plasticville watchman's shanty with crossing gate; set of railroad yard signs; 10 curved, 13 straight, 1008 camtrol, 1025 transformer.

Comments: Even though this was an exclusive Sears outfit that came in a set carton with Allstate graphics, it featured bargain basement contents. And what better way to glamorize them than by including plenty of track and a pair of switches? 1962 was the last year in which Lionel featured Plasticville accessories in their consumer catalogue. Mid-1960s Plasticville accessories that were included in Lionel outfits were packaged in either generic white boxes or, in this instance, Plasticville logo boxes. P. Ambrose Collection.   225   450

9810 / 19561   1966

Contents: 635 Union Pacific diesel switcher; 6014 white Frisco boxcar; 6465 orange Lionel Lines tank car;

The end of this 1966 Sears outfit box is very informative. It shows the Sears number as "SR 9808" and also shows the 19557 Lionel uncatalogued number. In addition to listing the contents, this set carton also illustrated the entire outfit. P. Ambrose Collection.

VG   LN

(6402) gray General-type flatcar with three pipes; 6176 black Lehigh Valley hopper; 346 manual culvert unloader with 6342 culvert pipe gondola; 6119-100 red/gray DL & W work caboose; Plasticville watchman's shanty with crossing gate; Plasticville train station; 11 curved, 23 straight, 6149, RH remote-control switch, 260 black plastic bumper, 1025 transformer.

Comments: This exclusive 1966 Sears outfit was packaged in an oversized outfit carton with Allstate graphics, and sold for $41.95. Both the Sears number, shown as "SR9810", and the 19561 Lionel uncatalogued set number were preprinted on the outfit box. At present, we cannot locate a Sears catalogue listing for this set. It was another outfit from the 1964-1966 era to include the 346 manual culvert unloader. Because of the special track plan, this outfit included an instruction sheet diagraming that plan. The sheet was numbered "19561" (the same as that which appeared on the set carton) and specifically notes a RH manual switch in contradiction to the remote-control switch listed on the outfit box. G. Metelak and J. Kerr Collections.

425   850

Exclusive Sears outfit 9813 was offered in their catalogue for $9.97; it was the least expensive postwar Lionel set they ever featured. Note the unique set carton with Allstate graphics that also lists the 19325 Lionel uncatalogued number. J. C. Penney also offered a similar low-end set in their 1964 catalogue as outfit 0664/19333. F. Davis Collection.

VG   LN

9813 / 19325   1964

Contents: 1061 steam locomotive; 1061T slope-back tender; (3309) turbo missile launcher; 6142 blue gondola with canisters; 6167 SP-type caboose; 110 trestle set; 12 curved, 6 straight; 1010 transformer.

Comments: This nonentity set was featured at $9.97 in the 1964 Sears Christmas catalogue. Even though inconsequential in content, many advanced collectors would be proud to own an example; low-end sets are difficult to obtain in collector condition. The set was packaged in an outfit carton with Allstate graphics and included the factory-printed 19325 Lionel uncatalogued number. Most interestingly, a similar set was offered in the 1964 J. C. Penney catalogue as outfit 0664/19333.

The Penney set was also packaged in a set carton with unique graphics, but it sold for $9.99 and did not include a trestle set! F. Davis Collection.   200   375

9820   1964

Contents: 240 steam locomotive; 242T streamlined tender; 3666 Minuteman boxcar with cannon; (6401-25) gray General-type flatcar with olive tank; 6470 exploding boxcar; (6824-50) first aid medical caboose; 347 cannon firing range set; packet of ten olive toy soldiers; 8 curved, 5 straight, 6149, 1025 transformer.

Comments: Besides being a Sears exclusive in an outfit carton with Allstate graphics, this is one of the most

Military-related 1964 outfit 9820 was a Sears exclusive and is one of the rarest and most highly sought of all postwar outfits. It was packaged in a set carton with Allstate Graphics, and included the first issue of the uncatalogued 240 Scout-series steam engine. Other rare items found with this set only are the 3666 cannon car with a light blue roof, a gray General-type flatcar with olive tank, and the unique 347 olive drab cannon firing range set. Note the inclusion of a packet of toy soldiers (shown at upper left) which is specifically mentioned on the side of the set carton. J. Algozzini Collection.

37

The 347 cannon firing range set is one of the rarest postwar accessories. It was modeled after the 448 missile range set, and Lionel never utilized the item again. The olive drab plastic battery has four cannon barrels which fire wooden silver projectiles. J. Algozzini Collection.

VG   LN

desirable, whether catalogued or uncatalogued, of any postwar Lionel train set. This outfit contained the first issue of the rare 240 engine and is the *only* set known to contain the 3666 cannon car, the flatcar with tank and the 347 cannon firing range set.

This outfit was planned early enough by Lionel in 1964 to be almost perfectly illustrated in the Sears Christmas catalogue. Only the engine was incorrectly depicted; it was shown as a 242 instead of with the correct 240 number. Note the number which we apply to the medical caboose; it is the correct *Lionel Service Manual* designation for the 6814 *without* accent pieces. We assume, also because of a *Service Manual* listing, that the -25 suffix listed with the 6401 flatcar is the correct number for the tank load. J. Algozzini Collection.   **1300   3000**

Pictured above are the four major variations of medical cabooses. Top left: Lionel catalogued version of the 6814 on a gray sheet metal chassis came with a full complement of accent pieces. Top right: This variation of the medical caboose was included in Sears outfit 9820. Although the caboose was also stamped "6814", it is referred to as "6824-50" in the Lionel Service Manual because of the open tool bin, i.e., lack of accent pieces. Note that the sheet metal chassis for 6824-50 is black rather than gray. Bottom left: The catalogued production version of the 6824 rescue unit, complete with accent pieces, came on an olive-painted sheet metal frame that was stamped "U.S.M.C.". Bottom right: The uncatalogued version of the olive rescue unit caboose was not numbered, and is referred to by the Lionel Service Manual listing (6119-125). It came with an open tool bin and was mounted on a black frame stamped "LIONEL". This caboose was a component of several uncatalogued sets, most notably 1964 J. C. Penney outfit 0680/19334. J. Algozzini Collection.

VG   LN

9834   1965

Contents: 237 steam locomotive; 242T streamlined tender; 6176 yellow Lehigh Valley hopper; 6822 night crew searchlight car; 346 manual culvert unloader with 6342 culvert pipe gondola; 6059 M St. L SP-type caboose; 14 curved, 11 straight, 6149, pair of manual switches, 1025 transformer.

Comments: The engine and rolling stock roster of this exclusive 1965 Sears outfit was identical to 1964 set 9807. However, the 321 trestle bridge and the 958 Plasticville vehicle set from the 1964 issue were eliminated from outfit 9834, yet both sets were priced the same at $29.99. This edition came in an oversized outfit carton, no longer elongated because the trestle bridge had been removed, with unique Allstate graphics. P. Michael Collection.   300   600

9835   1965

Contents: 216P/213T M St. L Alco AA units; 6014 Frisco boxcar; 6465 orange Lionel Lines tank car; 6176 black Lehigh Valley hopper; 6142 gondola with canisters; (6402) gray General-type flatcar with cable reels; 6059 M St. L SP-type caboose; 321 trestle bridge; 145 automatic gateman; three 76 street lamps; 17 curved, 22 straight, 1 half-straight, 6149, three manual switches, 260 bumper, 1073 transformer.

Comments: This is a marvelous and extremely scarce exclusive Sears outfit. It came packaged in an elongated, oversized outfit carton with Allstate graphics, and was catalogued by Sears as set 79 N 9835C, even though only "9835" appeared on the outfit box. However, the unique instruction sheet with track diagram that was included with this set was numbered "19454", which we assume was Lionel's corresponding uncatalogued outfit number used for costing purposes and production records.

The outfit carton proudly announced that "over 34 ft. of track" was included with this set, plus three switches. Aside from tremendous play value, this set was headed by the scarce uncatalogued 216 M St. L Alco unit. Note that the 216 power unit with weighted cab was paired with a non-weighted 213 dummy unit. This practice was also prevalent in the pairing of a weighted 215 Santa Fe power unit with a non-weighted 212 dummy. Weights were added to the cabs of some Alco power units to provide extra traction because Lionel ceased equipping their Alcos with Magnetraction after 1962. A. Tolli Collection.   500   1000

1965 outfit 9834 was a Sears exclusive. It was packaged in a special set carton with Allstate graphics. The manually operated culvert unloader was first issued through Sears as No. 346. Lionel later catalogued this unloader for separate sale and offered it in several promotional outfits other than those issued for Sears; in doing so, they relabeled existing inventory as "No. 348". Note that the 6342 culvert gondola included with this set was a factory error; it was stamped on only one side. P. Michael Collection.

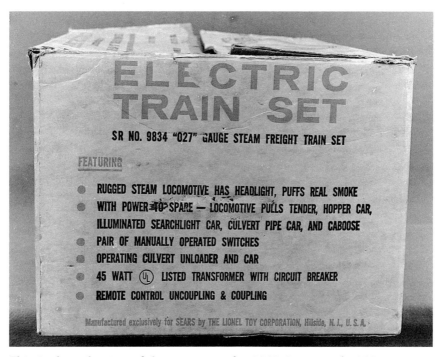

This is the side view of the set carton for 1965 Sears outfit 9834. It was common practice for the special Sears outfit boxes (those with Allstate graphics) to list the roster of contents. P. Michael Collection.

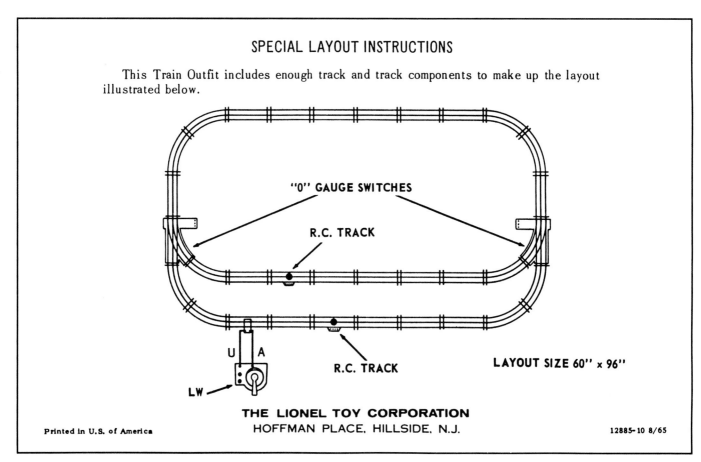

This was the unique layout instruction sheet included with Sears outfit 9836, headed by the rare 2347 C & O Geep. Note the number and date appearing in the bottom right-hand corner. Could 12885 be Lionel's outfit number for costing and record keeping purposes? Because this was an O Gauge set, and because Lionel used 12800-series outfit numbers for catalogued O Gauge sets in 1965, this is quite likely.

How to Assemble
LIONEL No. 321 TRESTLE BRIDGE

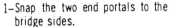

1—Snap the two end portals to the bridge sides.

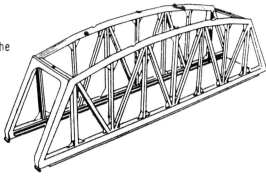

Clips on ends and top of bridge snap over pins molded on bridge sides. (Cement applied at these points will make the bridge more secure.)

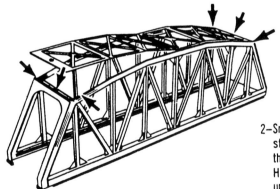

2—Snap on the two halves of the top structure and apply cement under the ends at the points indicated. Hold the ends down with a weight until the cement dries.

THE LIONEL TOY CORPORATION
HOFFMAN PLACE, HILLSIDE, N.J.

Printed in U.S. of America   321-101

This is the instruction sheet for the 321 trestle bridge that was included with outfit 9836. This variation of the bridge, without base plate, was not unique to the outfit, but is a scarce accessory. The proper accesssory box is numbered "321-100".

VG   LN

9836   **1965**

Contents: 2347 C & O Geep; 6415 Sunoco tank car; 6464-725 New Haven boxcar; 3662 operating milk car; 6414 auto loader; 346 manual culvert unloader with 6342 culvert pipe gondola; 6437 porthole caboose; 321-100 trestle bridge; three 76 street lamps; 10 curved, 18 straight, two UCS, pair of remote-control switches, LW transformer.

Comments: If a collector were given the choice of picking only one Sears outfit to own, this would probably be the one selected. This is the premier Sears postwar outfit, and instead of routine O27 offerings available in the 1960s, this set came with O Gauge track and, at $99.95, was as impressive as anything featured in the Lionel catalogue.

The uncatalogued 2347 C & O is one of the most prized postwar Lionel diesel engines. Its desirability alone on the collector market rivals that of some of the more highly sought F-3 units, and its value parallels that of the 2341 Jersey Central FM. The trestle bridge included with this set did *not* come with a metal base plate. Assembly was explained on a unique instruction sheet, and is numbered "321-100" on the original box, with no date given.

The outfit carton was an oversized conventional type with Allstate graphics, and contrary to the mid-1960s norm, all contents were component boxed. Be advised that the correct component box for the 2347 is a 2359 corrugated engine carton that was rubber stamped "2347" in either blue or black on a wider than usual piece of non-reinforced sealing tape. P. Beavin and P. Edward Collections.   **3500   6500**

Montgomery Ward

ANOTHER MIDWESTERN GIANT

Montgomery Ward, with national headquarters in Chicago, jumped on the Lionel bandwagon in the glory days of the mid-1950s when the Lionel name was still magic. Ward was on the scene and reaping the benefits of an association with Lionel long before Spiegel (1961) and J. C. Penney (1963); only Sears beat them to the well. Montgomery Ward's pricing offered value to the catalogue shopper. Though savings varied by outfit, their price averaged 15 to 20 percent less than Lionel's suggested retail price.

Because the authors have been able to examine only a very few of the uncatalogued sets discussed in this chapter, the Montgomery Ward catalogues have been the primary source of information. Unless specific mention of ownership is made at the end of a listing, it should be assumed by the reader that the Ward catalogue was the authors' source of information. We believe that Ward catalogue offerings of the 1950s were identical in content to Lionel catalogued sets, and that they were packaged in the same manner as the Lionel outfits. We also assume that most did *not* have a preprinted Ward outfit number. Quite possibly the only way to determine if a set came from Montgomery Ward is to search for other clues, such as a sales receipt or some type of store label affixed to the outside of the set carton. Unfortunately, such labels are likely to have become illegible with time. Also note that like Sears, Ward reused some outfit numbers for their catalogue listings.

The Montgomery Ward catalogue listings in this chapter are necessarily incomplete. The authors cannot find any catalogue listings of Lionel sets before 1955, and there is no Lionel information at all in the Ward catalogues for the years 1960 through 1965. In addition, there are no Ward listings for the years 1967-1969; Montgomery Ward may have "abandoned ship" as the Lionel name had lost much of its luster. Lionel did not issue a catalogue or manufacture any product in 1967, as explained in a letter sent to employees of Joe, the Motorists' Friend by the company's president (reprinted

in the chapter on 1967 in *Volume III*). In 1968 Lionel produced only one set, and by 1969 was experiencing its "last breath."

References to Lionel outfit numbering are frequently made in the text. Those that appear with a "/", such as 1525/500, are from the years 1955-1957 when Lionel issued the same catalogued outfits under two series of numbers. One or the other of those numbers appeared on the set carton, not both. A complete list of these correlating outfit numbers is given in *Volume III*, Appendix C.

Some fascinating bits of information about these uncatalogued sets have been uncovered. For example, Lionel issued some unique outfit boxes to Montgomery Ward, certainly in 1966 and possibly in some earlier years for which we currently lack data. As with Sears, some pricing disparities have been discovered in the nationally issued Ward catalogues. It is quite possible that separate regional catalogues were also issued during the postwar era, and that we have not yet unearthed them. For example, one 1958 catalogue issued in the Chicago area lists some prices ever so slightly lower than prices in a catalogue from another region. (Unfortunately, we cannot name the region because many years ago we photocopied only the pages pertaining to Lionel.) One wonders how prevalent was this practice of separate pricing—could it have been the norm for Montgomery Ward, or was 1958 an exception? Additional research will undoubtedly solve the puzzle.

In an effort to simplify the listings, as with the Spiegel and J. C. Penney chapters, the headings in this chapter will not show prefixes or suffixes. For instance, neither the 48 T and 48 HT prefixes nor the M suffix used by Montgomery Ward are shown, because they usually did *not* appear on the outfit carton, with 1966 being the only exception. The chart that follows, however, gives a complete listing of the inventory control numbers as they appeared in the Ward catalogues, along with the suggested retail prices.

Montgomery Ward Sets

Sets shown by year, with the complete catalogue stock number, the engine number, and the retail price.

Year	Catalogue Stock Number (Chicago Region)	Engine	Catalogue Price
1955	48 T 3000M	600	$16.95
1955	48 T 3001M	1615	$25.95
1955	48 T 3002M	2328	$33.45
1955	48 T 3003M	2016	$29.45
1955	48 T 3004M	2055	$42.95
1956	48 T 3018M	2338	$44.75
1956	48 T 3019M	2065	$44.95
1956	48 T 3030M	2018	$24.95
1956	48 T 3031M	621	$29.95
1957	48 T 3048M	628	$25.95
1957	48 T 3049M	250	$22.95
1957	48 T 3053M	2037	$32.95
1957	48 T 3058M	2037	$37.95
1958	48 T 3001M	249	$23.30
1958	48 T 3002M	210	$29.97
1958	48 T 3003M	2037	$36.97
1960	48 T 3073M	45	$29.97
1960	48 T 3074M	2018 or 2037	$39.97
1966	48 HT 21301	1062	$16.99
1966	48 HT 21302	237	$24.99

	VG	LN

3000 1955

Contents: 600 MKT diesel switcher; (6111) flatcar with logs; 6014 red Baby Ruth boxcar; 6017 SP-type caboose; 8 curved, 1 straight, 6029, 1014 transformer.

Comments: Even though the artist's rendering in the Ward catalogue was poor, this set corresponds to Lionel catalogued outfit 1525/500. Lionel had a suggested retail price of $19.95 in their literature while Ward offered the set for $16.95.

The 1955 Lionel consumer catalogue depicted sets ambiguously: Lionel did not list any sets by outfit number or give any suggested retail prices. Set numbers and pricing were obtained from advance dealer literature that was not available to the general public. **175 350**

3001 (multiple use of number) 1955

Contents: 1615 steam switcher; 1615T slope-back tender; 6462 red unpainted gondola with barrels; 6560 gray cab crane; 6119 red DL & W work caboose; 8 curved, 1 straight, 6029, 1014 transformer.

Comments: This outfit was identical to Lionel catalogued set 1527/502. Ward offered this set for $25.95 while Lionel suggested the retail at $29.95.

This outfit was also available through Sears as their outfit 9651. Page 241 of one regional edition of the 1955 Sears Christmas catalogue illustrated this outfit and priced it at $26.45, while another regional catalogue used the same price as Montgomery Ward, $25.95. Note that both the Ward and Sears catalogues incorrectly depict the crane as 6460, and to compound the error, the Ward catalogue incorrectly shows an artist's rendering of a 6419 work caboose instead of the 6119 with open tool bin. **350 600**

3001 (multiple use of number) 1958

Contents: 249 steam locomotive; 250T streamlined tender; 6112 gondola with canisters; 6424 flatcar with autos; 6014 Bosco or Frisco boxcar; 6810 flatcar with van; 6017 SP-type caboose; 957 Plasticville farm building and animal set; 12 curved, 4 straight, 1008 camtrol, 90° crossing, 1015 transformer.

Comments: Although this outfit consisted of standard 1958 Lionel catalogued items, it was offered in a roster that made it "A WARD EXCLUSIVE". Page 394 of the Montgomery Ward Christmas catalogue states "Save over 50% on special set—pieces sold individually would cost $51.80 in many stores". The authors reviewed two different 1958 Ward catalogues; the Chicago area catalogue listed the set price at $23.30 while another (area unknown) listed the price at $23.97.

This outfit included a Plasticville accessory, collectible in its own right. It also repeated the use of the 3001 inventory control number that was previously shown in the 1955 catalogue. **175 375**

3002 (multiple use of number) 1955

Contents: 2328 Burlington GP-7; 6462 red unpainted gondola with barrels; 6465 Sunoco tank car; 6456 black Lehigh Valley hopper; 6257 SP-type caboose; 8 curved, 3 straight, 6019, 1033 transformer.

Comments: This Ward set duplicates the Lionel catalogue offering of outfit 1531W/505. Ward priced the set at $33.45 while Lionel's suggested retail was $39.95. The 1955 Sears catalogue also featured the Burlington Geep, but it headed a slightly different freight roster. **425 800**

3002 (multiple use of number) 1958

Contents: 210P/210T Texas Special Alco AA units; 6801 flatcar with boat; 6014 orange Bosco boxcar; 6424 flatcar with autos; 6112 gondola with canisters; 6465 gray Gulf tank car; 6017 SP-type caboose; 8 curved, 3 straight, 6029, 1015 transformer.

Comments: This outfit also repeated a set number from the 1955 Ward catalogue. From the catalogue illustration we assume that this set is identical to Lionel's catalogued outfit 1599. The catalogue picture erroneously depicts 205 Missouri Pacific Alcos heading the outfit instead of the correct Texas Special units.

Although the 210 Alco pair was available in only one Lionel catalogued outfit, they are relatively common. They headed several uncatalogued sets including ones offered by Sears and Gifts Galore. Interestingly, this outfit was priced at $29.97 in two Ward catalogues published for different regions. **250 450**

3003 (multiple use of number) 1955

Contents: 2016 steam locomotive; 6026W square whistle tender; 6014 red Baby Ruth boxcar; 6012 gondola; 6017 SP-type caboose; 8 curved, 3 straight, 6029, 1033 transformer.

Comments: As shown in the Ward Christmas book, this set matches the Lionel catalogue listing for outfit 1000W/506. Lionel's suggested retail was $39.95 while Ward offered it for $29.45. An identical outfit was also featured in the Fall 1955 and Fall 1956 Sears catalogue, and it too was priced at $29.45.

The 2016 steam engine had neither smoke nor Magnetraction. It was a stripped-down version of the 2018, which itself was a stripped-down version of a 2037. The 2016 is far more scarce and much more collectible than either of the two previously mentioned engines. **300 500**

3003 (multiple use of number) 1958

Contents: 2037 steam locomotive; 6026W square whistle tender; 6424 flatcar with autos; 6014 Bosco or Frisco boxcar; 6818 flatcar with transformer; 6112 gon-

	VG	LN

dola with canisters; 6017 SP-type caboose; 8 curved, 3 straight, 6029, 1053 transformer.

Comments: This outfit was yet another Ward offering that duplicated a Lionel catalogued outfit, set 1603WS. This outfit also reused a number previously assigned in the 1955 Christmas book. Note that the Chicago area catalogue priced this set at $36.97 while another edition (from an unknown area) retailed it at $37.77. **250   475**

3004   1955

Contents: 2055 steam locomotive; 6026W square whistle tender; 3562-50 yellow operating barrel car; 6436 Lehigh Valley quad hopper; 6465 Sunoco tank car; 6357 illuminated SP-type caboose; 8 curved, 3 straight, 6019, 1033 transformer.

Comments: This Ward set was identical to the Lionel catalogued offering of outfit 1533WS/507. Lionel suggested that the set retail for $49.95, while Ward sold the outfit for $42.95. This set was also featured in the 1955 Sears Christmas catalogue as outfit 9653; the Chicago area edition listed the price at $43.45.

300   525

3018   1956

Contents: 2338 Milwaukee Road GP-7; 6430 flatcar with vans; 6462 red unpainted gondola with barrels; 6464-425 New Haven boxcar; 6346 Alcoa covered hopper; 6257 SP-type caboose; 8 curved, 3 straight, 6019, 1053 transformer.

Comments: This outfit corresponds to Lionel catalogued outfit 1553W/706. The 1956 Lionel catalogue intentionally omitted outfit numbers and retail prices; they had to be obtained from advance and dealer literature.

Contrary to the pricing of most of its other sets, Ward's retail of this outfit at $44.75 was only 10 percent less that the suggested Lionel price. Interestingly, this same set appears in the 1956 Sears catalogue as outfit 9613, priced at $44.75 and $44.95 in different regional issues. Lionel most assuredly advised each retailer that the other was featuring the set as a catalogued item, and to avoid embarrassment, suggested that each price the set similarly. **350   700**

3019   1956

Contents: 2065 steam locomotive; 6026W square whistle tender; 3424 Wabash brakeman; 6262 flatcar with wheels; 6562-25 red gondola with canisters; 6430 flatcar with vans; 6257 SP-type caboose; 8 curved, 3 straight, 6019, 1053 transformer.

Comments: This outfit was identical to Lionel catalogued set 1561WS/710. Ward offered the set for

	VG	LN

$44.95 while Lionel's suggested price for its retailers was $59.95.

There are two discrepancies on page 207 of the 1956 Ward Christmas book. The 6430 was shown with green Fruehauf vans instead of the correct Cooper-Jarrett vans, and the 3424 operating brakeman was shown in prototype form as a B & O Sentinel. Ward undoubtedly used the 1956 Lionel advance catalogue as the basis for their illustration, although the 1956 Lionel consumer catalogue correctly depicts both items. **425   725**

3030   1956

Contents: 2018 steam locomotive; 6026T square tender; (6121) flatcar with pipes; 6112 gondola with canisters; 6014 red Baby Ruth boxcar; 6257 SP-type caboose; 8 curved, 1 straight, 6029, 1015 transformer.

Comments: This Ward set duplicates the Lionel catalogue offering of outfit 1547S/702. There was no exclusivity on this set; facsimiles were also sold in 1956 by Firestone and Gifts Galore. **150   250**

3031   1956

Contents: 621 Jersey Central diesel switcher; 6362 rail truck car; 6425 Gulf tank car; 6562-25 red gondola with canisters; 6257 SP-type caboose; 8 curved, 3 straight, 6029, 1053 transformer.

Comments: This set as shown in the Ward Christmas book matches the Lionel catalogue listing for outfit 1551W/704. Lionel's suggested price was $39.95 while Ward offered the set for $29.95. The 621 Jersey Central is one of the more common mid-1950s diesel switchers. **300   500**

3048   1957

Contents: 628 Northern Pacific center cab; 6424 flatcar with autos; 6014 red Baby Ruth boxcar; 6025 black Gulf tank car; 6257 SP-type caboose; 10 curved, 5 straight, 6029, pair of manual switches, 1015 transformer.

Comments: The engine and rolling stock in this outfit correspond exactly to what was offered in 1956 Lionel catalogued outfit 1545/701, but differed in track content. Lionel's outfit contained a simple oval while this set included two additional straight sections and manual switches.

It appears that Lionel was left with unsold inventory on set 1545 and offered a "deal" to Montgomery Ward. The set undoubtedly had to be repackaged by Lionel because there was not an inch of unused space in outfit box 1545. Even though this outfit included a pair of switches that had a 1957 separate-sale price of $5.95, Ward sold it for $25.95, which was $4 less than the 1956 price suggested by Lionel. **175   325**

VG LN

3049   1957

Contents: 250 steam locomotive; 250T streamlined tender; 6424 flatcar with autos; (6121) flatcar with pipes; 6014-series boxcar; unknown boxcar; 6017 SP-type caboose; 12 curved, 4 straight, 1008 camtrol, 90° crossing, 1015 transformer.

Comments: We assume that this set was a Ward exclusive. As illustrated, it does not duplicate the Lionel catalogued offering of outfit 1573/727, which was the only catalogued set headed by the 250 Pennsylvania Scout series engine and tender.

The Ward catalogue states that this set contains two boxcars. We further assume that one was either a 6014-series Frisco or Bosco; the other may have been a 6024 Shredded Wheat or even a 6464-series O Gauge boxcar, which was used by Lionel as a component of six 1957 catalogued O27 Gauge outfits.   **200   375**

3053   1957

Contents: 2037 steam locomotive; 1130T streamlined tender; 6476 red Lehigh Valley hopper; (6121) flatcar with pipes; 6468-25 New Haven double-door boxcar; 6112 blue gondola with canisters; 6025 black Gulf tank car; (6111) flatcar with logs; 6017 SP-type caboose; 8 curved, 3 straight, 6029, 1043 transformer.

Comments: This outfit corresponds to the Lionel catalogued offering of 1579S/731. 1957 was the third consecutive year in which Lionel intentionally did not list outfit numbers or set prices; that information had to be obtained from advance and dealer literature. Ward pricing was indeed competitive; they priced the set at $32.95 while Lionel's suggested retail was $43.75.   **200   350**

3058   1957

Contents: 2037 steam locomotive; 6026W square whistle tender; 6482 refrigerator car; 6112 blue gondola with canisters; 6646 orange stock car; (6121) flatcar with pipes; 6476 Lehigh Valley hopper; 6017 SP-type caboose; 8 curved, 3 straight, 6029, 1053 transformer.

Comments: This outfit as shown in the Ward catalogue matches the Lionel catalogue roster for set 1583WS/733. It was one of the best O27 steam freight sets offered by any retailer in 1957 because it included the very collectible 6482 and 6646. They are two unappreciated and undervalued pieces of rolling stock, and are exceptionally scarce with component boxes.   **275   500**

3073   1960

Contents: 45 U.S.M.C. missile launcher; 3419 flatcar with operating helicopter; 6844 missile carrying flatcar; 3830 or 6830 flatcar with submarine; 6814 medical caboose; 12 curved, 3 straight, 6029, 90° crossing, 1053 transformer.

Comments: This outfit was noted in the catalogue as a special set exclusive to Montgomery Ward. Unfortunately, a description of the set box or data pertaining to component box packaging is unknown at this time. Furthermore, we cannot determine whether the flatcar with submarine is the operating 3830 or the non-operating 6830. Although all the contents were available in the 1960 Lionel catalogue, they were assembled here in a unique roster. Top-grade military/space-related outfits are difficult to obtain. The components were quite fragile and usually appear on the market in less than desirable condition.   **700   1300**

3074   1960

Contents: 2018 or 2037 steam locomotive; 6026W or 243W square whistle tender; 6825 flatcar with trestle; 6062 gondola with cable reels; 6470 exploding boxcar; 6650 flatcar with IRBM launcher; 6017 SP-type caboose; 10 curved, 5 straight, 6019, pair of manual switches, 1053 transformer.

Comments: This outfit, along with set 3073, was described as "Fast FLYING Trains for Jr. Engineers—Special Sets Exclusive at Ward". The rolling stock was regular issue from the 1960 Lionel product line, but the engine that fronted this outfit is in question. A 2018 is shown in the Ward catalogue, but because the set included a whistle tender, it seems likely that a 2037 may have headed this set. The 2018 was paired with a whistle tender by Lionel only once, in 1956 catalogued outfit 1555WS.   **275   475**

21301 / 19542   1966

Contents: 1062 (2-4-2) steam locomotive; 1062T slope-back tender; 6465 orange Lionel Lines tank car; (6408) flatcar with pipes; 6167 SP-type caboose; trestle set; eight-piece yard sign set; 12 curved, 6 straight, 1008 camtrol, 1025 transformer.

Comments: This set with unassuming contents was shown on page 352 of the 1966 *Talk of the Town* Christmas catalogue. It was a Ward exclusive and came in a unique orange conventional outfit box with Montgomery Ward logo. Information was given on the top of the carton and on all four sides. Note that this outfit box showed the Ward inventory control number, printed as "48-21301", and the five-digit Lionel uncatalogued number 19542.

The trestle set prompts some interesting commentary. As Lionel catalogue number 110, it came with 24 (1950s-early 1960s) and 22 (mid-1960s) graduated piers. The text in the Ward catalogue stated only "16 graduated trestles"! Was this a misprint or did Lionel package a special set of trestles with only sixteen piers? D. Cirillo Collection.   **225   375**

This unique Montgomery Ward outfit box was for Ward's exclusive 1966 catalogued set 48-21301. Note that the set carton was also marked with the Lionel uncatalogued outfit number 19542. At the present time, the authors are aware of only two Ward sets that came packaged in a set carton with Montgomery Ward graphics; the other was companion 1966 outfit 21302. D. Cirillo Collection.

	VG	LN

21302 / 19544   1966

Contents: 237 steam locomotive; 242T streamlined tender; 3362/64 operating log car; 6014 white Frisco boxcar; 6176 black Lehigh Valley hopper; 6167 SP-type caboose; eight-piece rail and road sign set, Plasticville suburban station and signal bridge; 12 curved, 7 straight, 6149, 90° crossing, 1025 transformer.

Comments: This was a Montgomery Ward exclusive that came in a unique outfit box with Ward logo, and with information and illustrations on the top and all four sides. It was priced at $24.99, and the rolling stock was quite similar to catalogued outfit 11520.

The engine and rolling stock included with this outfit were typical items from the 1966 product line, but the inclusion of the various Plasticville items makes this set intriguing. We are not aware of any specific packaging done by Plasticville (Bachmann Brothers) for Lionel in the mid-1960s; therefore, we assume that the Plasticville items were packaged in Plasticville or generic white boxes. In the late 1950s and early 1960s, however, Bachmann Brothers did package items specially for Lionel. Orange and blue boxes with preprinted Lionel graphics were shipped to Bachmann in Philadelphia; Bachmann then packaged the appropriate Plasticville items in the Lionel boxes and returned them to Lionel ready for distribution. L. Harold Collection.   **250   425**

Spiegel

CHICAGO'S OTHER PARTICIPANT

Spiegel is another of the Chicago-based retailers. Even though the lion's share of their revenue was generated via mail order, they did operate company stores. They were at the second tier of mail-order retailing during the 1960s, dwarfed in sales volume by the giants, namely Sears Roebuck and Montgomery Ward.

Lionel was never the superstar of the Spiegel catalogue and was not even introduced to it until 1961. (American Flyer and Marx shared top billing in the late 1940s, while Marx was the preeminent name featured in the 1950s.) A fascinating question arises—who solicited whom? (Lionel appears to have temporarily lost Montgomery Ward as a customer in 1961. One wonders if Lionel's courting of Spiegel caused that loss. If there were other reasons for losing Ward, perhaps Lionel was forced to pursue Spiegel to fill the sales vacuum.) For whatever reason, we assume that Lionel came knocking at Spiegel's door with a sales pitch too good to be refused. Unless Spiegel was given favorable pricing and liberal return privileges, why would they bother with Lionel trains? Sales on toy trains were ebbing by the late 1950s, and Lionel's impact on Spiegel's sales volume in the 1960s had to be absolutely minimal.

There are very few sets that can be definitely attributed to Spiegel and, for that reason, most of our research data has been taken from their catalogues rather than actual sets. The only listings that the authors have actually seen are those that include the collector's name. Spiegel issued numerous catalogues; there were fall catalogues, winter catalogues, fall-winter issues, newsstand editions, and Christmas catalogues. It is possible that variations of each catalogue may have been printed for different regions of the continental United States. Lionel trains usually appeared in the Christmas editions of their catalogues, and were shown without interruption from 1961 through 1967. The authors had the good fortune to review an abundance of Spiegel catalogues from the beginning of the postwar era through 1969. Our only disappointment has been the year 1964; we have not yet been able to locate any catalogues from that year.

The Lionel items that were shown in the Spiegel catalogues were far from the top-of-the-line, quality merchandise that made the Lionel name renowned. In most instances, some of Lionel's least expensive products were presented. Nonetheless, the mail-order shopper realized measurable savings by purchasing through Spiegel. Their catalogue pricing afforded savings of about 20 percent when compared to the same or similar merchandise purchased through Lionel dealers.

Illustrations in the Spiegel catalogue were vague. Seldom were track and transformer well described, and the listings never told whether steam engines were plastic or die cast. All Spiegel sets were prefaced in their catalogues by "R 36 J". An identical preface or a variation of it *sometimes* appeared on the set carton. We assume that most outfit boxes were numbered in some way with both Spiegel and Lionel outfit numbers, but the Lionel number, from either the catalogued or uncatalogued sequence, always appeared on the box. Just as with Sears and Montgomery Ward, there was multiple use of some outfit numbers by Spiegel in their catalogues. Because the same "R 36 J" prefix was a constant in their catalogue listings, we have deleted it from the headings in the text. A chronological chart included with this chapter, however, gives the complete Spiegel inventory control number along with the suggested retail price.

Spiegel Sets

Sets shown by year, with the complete catalogue stock number, the engine number, and the retail price.

Year	Catalogue Stock Number	Engine	Catalogue Price
1961	R36 J 5260	246?	$19.94
1961	R36 J 5261	233	$29.33
1961	R36 J 5263	218	$38.88
1962	R36 J 5276	229	$38.88
1962	R36 J 5277	233	$29.87
1962	R36 J 5278	242	$18.87
1963	R36 J 5285	211	$29.84
1963	R36 J 5286	237	$23.94
1963	R36 J 5287	221 Rio Grande	$17.94
1964	R36 J 5284	237	Unknown
1965	R36 J 5261	1062	$14.97
1965	R36 J 5262	237	$19.97
1965	R36 J 5263	215	$24.97
1966	R36 J 5258	1062	$14.77
1966	R36 J 5259	1062	$19.97
1966	R36 J 5260	215	$27.97
1967	R36 J 5266	200-Series Steam	$19.97

VG   LN

5258   1966

Contents: 1062 steam locomotive; 1061T slope-back tender; 6142 gondola without load; 6176 Lehigh Valley hopper; 6167 SP-type caboose; 8 curved, 2 straight, 1008 camtrol, 1010 transformer.

Comments: This starter outfit was priced at $14.77, the lowest ever in the Spiegel catalogue for a Lionel set. It was about as basic a set as one could get, and still have an engine with a motor. The 6142 gondola usually had a load of two unstamped canisters or two empty cable reels; the example illustrated with this outfit had no load whatsoever.   **75   125**

5259   1966

Contents: 1062 steam locomotive; 1062T slope-back tender; 3362/3364 operating log car; 6014 white Frisco boxcar; 6176 black Lehigh Valley hopper; 6167 SP-type caboose; 12 curved, 7 straight, 6149, 90° crossing, 1025 transformer.

Comments: This outfit is nothing more than another run-of-the-mill, low-end steam freight set. Spiegel priced the set at $19.97 while a comparable starter set, outfit 11520 as illustrated in the 1966 Lionel consumer catalogue, was retailed for $22.50. The black and white Spiegel illustration of the engine appears to be a 1062, but because of the 2-4-2 wheel alignment, it could possibly be a 242. Note that the eight straight sections of track included with this set was more than Lionel packaged with their top-of-the-line 1966 catalogued O Gauge outfit.   **75   150**

5260 (multiple use of number)   1961

Contents: 246? steam locomotive; 244T slope-back tender; 6050 Lionel savings bank car; 3330 flatcar with submarine in kit form; 6017 SP-type caboose; track and transformer unknown.

Comments: This set was advertised in the 1961 catalogue as a Spiegel exclusive, and was the *first* Lionel product to appear in a Spiegel catalogue. It was indistinctly pictured, and even though the catalogue gave no track information, it mentioned "with circuit breaker transformer", which was probably a 1010. We assume the engine was a 246 because it was described as having Magnetraction and headlight. The 3330 is a scarce and collectible item, and at the separate-sale price of $7.95, was an expensive car to be included in an uncatalogued set, especially one that sold for only $19.94.

     200   375

5260 / 19507 (multiple use of number)   1966

Contents: 215P/212T Santa Fe Alco AA units; 6176 Lehigh Valley hopper; 6142 gondola with canisters; 6465 orange Lionel Lines tank car; 6050 Swift savings bank car; 6059 M St. L SP-type caboose; 12 curved, 7 straight, 6149, 90° crossing, 1073 transformer.

Comments: This outfit was almost identical to 1965 Spiegel set 5263, but included one additional rolling stock item along with extra track. It was retailed in their catalogue for $27.97. The Spiegel outfit came with unboxed contents in a tan conventional two-tier carton that included the Lionel number "19507" along with the Spiegel inventory control number printed as "36 J 5260". Identical contents surface in a Type D display-style set box as Lionel uncatalogued outfit 19506; this set was also available from other retailers, and through the 1966 J. C. Penney catalogue as set 8279 for $28.88. C. Vegazo Collection.   **175   350**

5261 (multiple use of number)   1961

Contents: 233 steam locomotive; 233W square whistle tender; 6162 gondola with canisters; 6343 barrel ramp car; 6476 Lehigh Valley hopper; 6017 SP-type caboose; 8 curved, 4 straight, 1008 camtrol, 147 whistle controller, 1073 transformer.

Comments: From the catalogue illustration it appears that this set is the same as Lionel catalogued outfit 1646. *Volume III* shows a color photograph of this outfit on page 125. The Spiegel price for this set was $29.33 while the retail price suggested by Lionel for its dealers was $39.95.   **150   250**

5261 (multiple use of number)   1965

Contents: 1062 steam locomotive; 1062T slope-back tender; 6142 gondola with canisters; (6402) gray General-type flatcar with cable reels; 6059 M St. L SP-type caboose; 12 curved, 3 straight, 6149, 90° crossing, 1010 transformer.

Comments: At $14.97 in the Spiegel catalogue, this outfit was one of the least expensive Lionel sets offered, and it was about as bland as any set imaginable. All components were run-of-the-mill items from the mid-1960s and have virtually no collector value. This outfit reused an inventory control number that had been previously assigned in 1961.   **75   125**

5262   1965

Contents: 237 steam locomotive; 1062T slope-back tender; (6402) gray General-type flatcar with cable reels; 6142 gondola with canisters; 6014 white Frisco boxcar; 6059 M St. L SP-type caboose, 12 curved, 3 straight, 6149, 90° crossing, 1010 transformer.

VG   LN

Comments: This outfit was a Spiegel exclusive, but there was nothing exclusive about the contents: they were a rather basic mixture of common items from the mid-1960s. Because this set was exclusive to Spiegel, it *may* exist in an outfit box with a special logo. Unique set boxes for exclusive outfits were made available to Sears, Ward and Penney during the same time period. The 237 engine fronted Lionel catalogued sets in 1963 and 1964. By 1965 it was probably significantly overstocked, and also appeared in both Ward and J. C. Penney outfits. Note that 1965 Penney outfit 3726 was identical to this set, except for the substitution of a streamlined tender.   **100   175**

5263 (multiple use of number)   **1961**

Contents: 218P/218C Santa Fe Alco AB units; 6343 barrel ramp car; 6445 Ft. Knox car; 6475 pickle vat car;

VG   LN

6405 flatcar with van; 6017 SP-type caboose; 8 curved, 4 straight, 1008 camtrol, 1063 transformer.

Comments: This outfit was identical to Lionel catalogued set 1649, and was the best O27 Gauge diesel freight set that Lionel offered in 1961. The suggested price for Lionel's dealers was $49.95, while the Spiegel catalogue retailed the set for $38.88, a savings of more than 20 percent. 1961 was the first year in which Lionel trains appeared in the Spiegel catalogue; maybe this outfit was one of the perquisites which Lionel used to gain entry to Spiegel's market.   **400   750**

5263 (multiple use of number)   **1965**

Contents: 215P/212T Santa Fe Alco AA units; 6142 gondola with canisters; 6465 orange Lionel Lines tank car;

This outfit was a Spiegel exclusive and is dated to 1962. It positively identifies a Lionel uncatalogued set number in the 19100 series, and more importantly, it lists the Spiegel inventory control number, printed as "36-J-5278". This dual-numbered outfit had both numbers printed on the carton by Lionel before the set was shipped from the factory. Outfit boxes that included a preprinted Spiegel set number are few and far between. P. Michael Collection.

VG LN

6176 Lehigh Valley hopper; 6130 Santa Fe work caboose; 12 curved, 3 straight, 6149, 90° crossing, 1025 transformer.

Comments: The Philadelphia edition of the 1965 Spiegel catalogue shows this outfit on page 375 with a retail price of $24.97. Analysis reveals contents identical to those listed and photographed as set 19444 in the chapter on General Retailers in this book. Please refer to that listing for additional comments; also review 1966 Spiegel outfit 5260.   **175   350**

5266   1967

Contents: 200 Scout-series steam locomotive; 1060T or 242T streamlined tender; 6465 orange Lionel Lines tank car; 6176 Lehigh Valley hopper; 6473 rodeo car; 6119-100 red/gray DL & W work caboose; 8 curved, 1 straight, 6149, 1025 transformer.

Comments: Unfortunately, the catalogue illustration on page 418 of the 1967 edition of the Spiegel Christmas catalogue so poorly depicts the engine that we

Lionel's 1964 outfit 19371 may have been available to various merchants, but the example shown here was purchased at a Spiegel store in downtown Chicago. Although the contents were ordinary, a large proof of purchase sticker (form 3492 Rev 4-63) numbered "47639" was affixed over the Lionel name. An additional sticker marked "Spiegel Inc./35th St. Store", which functioned as a sales receipt, was placed on top of the set carton and positively identified Spiegel as the retailer. Although not shown in this photograph (see black and white photo on page 54), the Spiegel inventory control number, printed as "36 5284", was rubber stamped by Spiegel on the side of the outfit carton. R. Sylvan Collection.

VG   LN

are unable to positively identify it. Clearly it is from the 200 Scout series but could be any number from leftover 1966 inventory; possibilities include 237, 239 (die-cast), 242, or even the rare uncatalogued die-cast 241 or 251. The 239 is the most likely because the consist of this outfit is identical to 1966 Lionel catalogued set 11540. Spiegel catalogue listings never mention whether the steam engines were plastic or die-cast; other retail store listings are much more helpful and descriptive. Chances are that this set may surface with different engines. Remember that there was no production for 1967 and that Lionel did not issue a catalogue for that year. They were "house cleaning" in anticipation of their move to Hagerstown, Maryland. *Volume III* further explains Lionel's situation at the time in the chapter entitled "1967 — The Black Hole". **125   200**

5276   1962

Contents: 229P/229C M St. L Alco AB units; (3413) Mercury capsule launcher; (6512) cherry picker car; 6413 Mercury capsule carrier; 6463 rocket fuel tank car; 6059 red M St. L SP-type caboose; 8 curved, 4 straight, 1008 camtrol, 147 horn controller, 1073 transformer.

Comments: This Spiegel outfit appears to duplicate Lionel catalogued set 11288. Lionel suggested its dealers retail the outfit at $49.95 while the Spiegel price was considerably less—$38.88. This outfit, whether purchased through Spiegel or another retailer, has been shown to be one of the best sets produced by Lionel in 1962; the rolling stock was all new for the product year and is both collectible and extremely fragile. **650   1200**

5277   1962

Contents: 233 steam locomotive; 233W or 243W square whistle tender; 3357 cop and hobo car; 6405 flatcar

This is the side view of Spiegel set 5284 (please see color photo on page 53). Note the Spiegel inventory control number "36 5284". R. Sylvan Collection.

VG   LN

with van; 6062 gondola with cable reels; 6057 SP-type caboose; 8 curved, 4 straight, 1008 camtrol, 147 whistle controller, 1073 transformer.

Comments: This was the second year in which Spiegel catalogued an outfit headed by a 233 engine. At $29.87, the 1962 version was priced pennies higher than the earlier one and also offered a four-unit rolling stock roster. This outfit rates slightly better than the similar 5261 because the 6405 and 3357 have been shown to be more desirable freight cars in the collector market.

175   300

5278 / 19185   1962

Contents: 242 steam locomotive; 1060T streamlined tender; (3349) turbo missile launcher; 6448 exploding boxcar; 6057 SP-type caboose; 8 curved, 4 straight, 1008 camtrol, 1010 transformer.

Comments: This outfit was a Spiegel exclusive and contained a collectible roster of military/space-related rolling stock. The outfit box was a tan conventional two-tier type in which the contents were separated by cardboard dividers. Both the Lionel stock number 19185 and the Spiegel inventory control number, rubber stamped as "36-J-5278", appear on the end of the set box. P. Michael Collection. **125   225**

5284 / 19371   1964

Contents: 237 steam locomotive; 1060T streamlined tender; 6465 orange Lionel Lines tank car; 6142 green gondola with canisters; 6014 white Frisco boxcar; 6473 rodeo car; 6017 SP-type caboose; track and transformer unknown.

Comments: This set came with unboxed contents in a conventional white two-tier outfit box that had both the Spiegel retail stock number and the corresponding uncatalogued Lionel set number stamped on the box; the Lionel number 19371 was printed at the factory on the end of the box while the Spiegel number, rubber stamped as "36 5284", appeared on the side of the carton. Even though we cannot locate a catalogue listing (this may have been a special regional issue), we know that the outfit is dated to 1964 because of the 19300-series number and the set box. The white generic set carton with orange lettering was introduced by Lionel in 1964, but was most often reserved for O Gauge outfits. R. Sylvan Collection.

125   225

5285   1963

Contents: 211P/211T Texas Special Alco AA units; 6465-110 Cities Service tank car; 6440 flatcar with vans; (6469) liquefied gas car; 6822 night crew searchlight car; 6414 auto loader; 6257-100 SP-type caboose with stack; 8 curved, 3 straight, 6139, 1025 transformer.

VG   LN

Comments: By 1963 standards, this could be considered a very good set; the rolling stock has proved to be some of the most collectible that Lionel ever offered. The 6469 is an extremely desirable item, while the 1963 issue of the 6414 auto loader has been known to contain the exceptionally scarce "cheap" autos—those without bumpers, wheels or windshields. Even the 6257 caboose piques interest because it is a moderately scarce example with a die-cast smokestack. The 211 Alco units, which were previously numbered "210", were reintroduced by Lionel in 1962.   700   1300

5286   **1963**

Contents: 237 steam locomotive; 1060T streamlined tender; 6050 Swift savings bank car; 6465 orange Lionel Lines tank car; (6408) flatcar with pipes; 6162 gondola with canisters; 6119-100 red/gray DL & W work caboose; 8 curved, 1 straight, 6139, 1025 transformer.

Comments: This set was identical to Lionel catalogued outfit 11351. It was priced at $23.94, while the retail price suggested by Lionel for its dealers was $26.95. Although the 237 engine was offered in only two catalogued sets, it appears frequently in uncatalogued

VG   LN

outfits. Except for the 6408, there is nothing of collector interest offered with this outfit.   125   200

5287   **1963**

Contents: 221 Rio Grande Alco A unit; 3410 flatcar with operating helicopter; (6407) flatcar with rocket; 6014 white Frisco car; 6463 rocket fuel tank car; 6059 M St. L SP-type caboose; 8 curved, 1 straight, 6149, 1010 transformer.

Comments: At first glance, this outfit does not look very impressive, but because of the inclusion of the 6407, it commands respect. The 6407 is the rarest and most valued of the military/space-related rolling stock. Reproductions of the rocket and nose cone (both marked and unmarked) are widely available in the marketplace; extreme caution is advised.

Except for the substitution of the 221 Rio Grande for the 634 diesel switcher, this set mirrors Lionel catalogued outfit 11341. The most probable reason for this substitution is that J. C. Penney featured the identical Lionel catalogued outfit in their 1963 catalogue as set 4881!

650   1200

J. C. Penney

THE EAST COAST CONNECTION

With headquarters in New York City, J. C. Penney was a late arrival, not appearing on the scene until 1963, long after the Lionel pendulum began its downswing. (Sears and Spiegel were still active customers while Montgomery Ward seemed to be in a temporary hiatus during the early 1960s.) Again we pose the question — Who solicited whom? Because Lionel was desperate for business, we assume that *they* approached J. C. Penney on their knees. In the early 1950s, the Lionel salesman was regarded almost as a deity, one who was afforded every courtesy; his business card was like a magical key, opening almost any door. Lionel trains were the life blood of many retailers, and merchants tried desperately to remain in the salesman's good favor so as not to jeopardize their precious allotment of trains. By the 1960s, that formerly celebrated person had become just another salesman. No longer were appointments made at his convenience. He was forced to rely on phone solicitation that more often than not fell on deaf ears; he was further humbled by being made to wait in line for appointments with toy buyers. The one-time god-like figure became just another mortal human being forced to take "No" for an answer.

Accumulating and analyzing data from the J. C. Penney catalogues and archives, our primary references for this chapter, has been a herculean task. Like the other major mail-order retailers, J. C. Penney most assuredly published several editions of their national catalogue, and printed regional catalogues and employed regional purchasing agents (refer to the introduction of the Sears chapter for expanded information). Furthermore, some outfits were probably retailed over-the-counter in larger Penney outlets and were *never* shown in their catalogues.

A J. C. Penney's representative stated that their catalogue division was not created until 1963; hence there are no listings prior to that year. In addition, we have no Penney listings for the years 1967 and 1968. Remember that Lionel did not publish a catalogue or manufacture any product in 1967; they were in a state of turmoil, and in the process of regrouping and moving the manufacturing portion of their operation to Hagerstown, Maryland. When production resumed in 1968, Lionel catalogued only one outfit.

As in the other chapters, the J. C. Penney outfits are listed in numerical sequence rather than by year of issue. In order to simplify the listings, the X900 series prefix and the letter A suffix have been deleted. We have, however, given a listing of the complete J. C. Penney catalogue stock numbers along with the suggested retail price in the chart that follows. Be advised that some catalogues may exist with pricing that is different from what is listed in the chart.

While reviewing the chart, pay particular attention to the suggested retail prices. J. C. Penney's pricing structure, as a rule of thumb, was about 25 percent less than corresponding or comparable Lionel catalogued outfits. Money could certainly be saved by shopping through the J. C. Penney catalogue.

For identification purposes, most of the Penney outfits that we have examined have nothing more than a small price sticker showing the Penney inventory control number affixed somewhere on the set carton. To the best of our knowledge, the only outfit that was packaged in a unique set carton with J. C. Penney logo was 1964 set 0664. It appears that Penney accepted Lionel train sets at all other times in ordinary Lionel-issued boxes. Some of the listings in this volume make no reference to either outfit boxes or packaging simply because we have not observed them first hand. Unless a collector's name is given at the end of a listing, it is to be assumed by the reader that the information given for that listing was derived from a J. C. Penney catalogue. Please see Chart V in the Prologue for a complete description of O27 Gauge outfit boxes. Like Montgomery Ward and Spiegel, the J. C. Penney sets are indeed fertile ground for future study.

J. C. Penney Sets

Sets shown by year, with the complete catalogue stock number, the engine number, and the retail price.

Year	Catalogue Stock Number	Engine	Catalogue Price
1963	X 923-4782 A	238	$29.98
1963	X 923-4881 A	634	$18.88
1963	X 923-4899 A	237	$22.95
1964	X 924-0664 A	1062	$9.99
1964	X 924-0672 A	223	$18.88
1964	X 924-0680 A	221 U.S.M.C.	$13.88
1965	X 924-3700 A	2322	$69.99
1965	X 924-3718 A	241?	$34.44
1965	X 924-3726 A	237	$18.99
1965	X 924-3734 A	241	$29.00
1966	X 924-8261 A	237	$19.88
1966	X 924-8279 A	215	$28.88
1966	X 924-8287 A	241	$37.77
1969	X 926-1082 A	1061	$19.99
1969	X 926-1090 A	2041	$34.50

The question mark (?) indicates that confirmation is needed.

0664 / 19333   1964

Contents: 1062 steam locomotive; 1060T streamlined Southern Pacific tender; (6502) flatcar with girder; 6176 Lehigh Valley or 6076 ATSF hopper; (6167) red unstamped SP-type caboose; 12 curved, 4 straight, 90° crossing, 1010 transformer.

Comments: This set was advertised in the 1964 Christmas catalogue as "Now... A Penney Exclusive!" It may have been exclusive to J. C. Penney, but it was extremely low end and was priced at only $9.99. Most interestingly, this outfit came in a set carton with unique J. C. Penney graphics, and was also marked with the 19333 Lionel uncatalogued set number.

The Southern Pacific tender and the ATSF hopper were originally issued as part of the Libby promotional outfit 19263 in 1963, and here they appear in a Penney set; that does not say much for exclusivity as per the catalogue hype. Another collectible variation was some-

times included with this set; instead of an orange girder, the 6502 flatcar also came with a black girder with "LIONEL" markings. S. Bradley, P. Michael and J. Algozzini Collections.   **200   375**

0672   1964

Contents: 223P/212T Santa Fe Alco AA units; 3362/3364 operating log car; 6473 rodeo car; 6142 gondola with cable reels; 6059 M St. L SP-type caboose; 12 curved, 3 straight, 6149, 147 whistle controller, 1010 transformer.

Comments: The inclusion of the 223 Santa Fe Alco makes this is a very collectible outfit. The 223 was paired with a 218C to head 1963 Lionel catalogued outfit 11385. By 1964 it had become overstocked inventory and was paired with a 212T, a new number in the Santa Fe series. This was done because all 223 cabs had a weight added for traction while the 212T cabs did not; there was no

Pictured above is an exclusive J. C. Penney outfit that was featured in their 1964 Christmas catalogue as set 924-0664 A for the unbelievably low price of $9.99. This is the only Penney set that we are aware of that came in an outfit carton with unique Penney graphics. Note that the outfit box was also marked with the 19333 Lionel uncatalogued set number. In the foreground, we are showing the contents as purchased on the resale market with a Southern Pacific tender and an unstamped 6167 SP-type caboose. However, the catalogue illustration featured a Lionel Lines tender and a 6059 M St. L caboose that, for reference only, are shown in the background. This was the lowest priced Lionel set ever featured in the J. C. Penney catalogue. Be advised that Sears featured a similar low-end set in their 1964 catalogue as outfit 9813. J. Algozzini Collection.

VG   LN

reason to include a weighted cab in a dummy unit. This reasoning also led to the pairing of weighted 215P units with 212Ts. Note that the 3364, which is merely a 3362 with logs, did not appear in the Lionel catalogue until 1965.

This set with its $18.88 price tag was an exceptional value. The comparable catalogued Lionel outfit 11480 headed by a 213 AA Alco pair without a horn was priced at $34.95.   **275   550**

0680 / 19334   1964

Contents: 221 U.S.M.C. Alco A unit; (6176-100) olive drab hopper; (6142) olive drab gondola; (3309) olive drab turbo missile launcher; (6119-125) olive drab work caboose; packet of 12 olive drab toy soldiers; 8 curved, 1 straight, 6149, 1010 transformer.

Comments: This is one of the best of the postwar uncatalogued sets. Every item in the set is in collector demand. It came packaged in a Type D display-style outfit box with orange and white 1964 graphics. The ends of the set carton lid were rubber stamped with the Lionel un-

catalogued number "19334". Except for the catalogue illustration, the only way of knowing that this set was purchased through J. C. Penney is a tiny price sticker that was printed with both the Penney inventory control number and the retail price.

The J. C. Penney catalogue touted this outfit as "Lionel 'O27'-Gauge Troop-Train Set", and included the toy soldiers for additional play value. The rolling stock came with one fixed and one operating coupler; the olive drab 3309 is exceptionally scarce. Contrary to the catalogue illustration of a Santa Fe Alco unit with an open pilot, all examples of this set that we have verified came with an olive drab 221 U.S.M.C. engine. The outfit is priced here with the U.S.M.C. unit, which is considerably more common than the exceptionally scarce 221 olive drab Santa Fe. Even though this outfit is documented in our Penney literature as set 924-0680 at $13.88, the price sticker on the example illustrated in this book shows it as outfit 923-5361 at $14.88 retail! To account for this discrepancy, we must assume that this set was also offered in some regional catalogue, perhaps in early 1964, or sold over-the-counter at a J. C. Penney store. At either $13.88 or $14.88, this was the second lowest-priced Lionel set

This is one of the best uncatalogued sets offered by any retailer during the postwar era. It was shown in the 1964 J. C. Penney catalogue as set 0680, while Lionel numbered the outfit 19334. The only way of knowing this set was purchased through J. C. Penney was a miniature price sticker also printed with the Penney inventory control number. Even though this outfit is documented in our Penney literature as set 924-0680 at $13.88, the price sticker on the example illustrated lists this as outfit 923-5361 at $14.88 retail! We must assume that this set was also offered in some regional catalogue, perhaps in early 1964 because of the 923 prefix, or sold over the counter at a J. C. Penney store. V. Bibelot Collection.

VG   LN

that Penney catalogued, but it is the most valuable of their outfits on the collector market today. V. Bibelot Collection.

1200 2200

1082   1969

Contents: 1061 (2-4-2) steam locomotive; 1061T slope-back tender; (6402) gray General-type flatcar with cable reels; 6142 green gondola with canisters; 6059 red M St. L SP-type caboose; 8 curved, 2 straight, 1025 transformer.

Comments: As depicted in the J. C. Penney catalogue, this outfit was identical to Lionel catalogued outfit 11710. It was priced at $19.99 while the 1969 Lionel consumer catalogue gave no prices.

The 1969 edition of the 1061 engine was offered with a 2-4-2 wheel configuration rather than an 0-4-0 of earlier issues. Even though this set did not include an uncoupling section, the rolling stock was usually equipped with one fixed and one operating coupler. The Lionel factory underwent a major house-cleaning in 1969, and set components varied more than in any previous year. Many 1969 components were fitted with the odd combination of late AAR trucks with operating couplers, paired with arch bar trucks with fixed couplers. **75 125**

1090   1969

Contents: 2041P/2041T Rock Island Alco AA units; 6315 Gulf chemical tank car; 6142 blue gondola with canisters; 6014 white Frisco boxcar; 6476 yellow Lehigh Valley hopper; (6057) unstamped SP-type caboose; 8 curved, 7 straight, 6149, 1025 transformer.

Pictured here is the J. C. Penney set 1090, one of two identical Lionel catalogued outfits that was also featured in the 1969 Penney catalogue. Lionel was in serious financial trouble in 1969, and catalogued a total of only six outfits. P. Ambrose Collection.

VG   LN

Comments: The catalogue illustration of this outfit was identical to Lionel catalogued outfit 11740. It was priced at $34.50 while the Lionel consumer catalogue gave no prices.

The 1969 Lionel product line was dismal; the 2041 Alco was a disappointment when compared to the fine-quality Alcos of the early 1950s. The 6315 was catalogued as Lionel Lines, but usually had the scarce Gulf markings. Once separated from the set, none of the items are difficult to obtain. The key to this set is the outfit box itself. P. Ambrose Collection. **225 400**

3700   1965

Contents: 2322 Virginian FM; 3662 operating milk car; 6361 timber transport car; 6464-725 New Haven boxcar; 6436-110 Lehigh Valley quad hopper; 6315 Lionel Lines chemical tank car; 6822 night crew searchlight car; 6437 Pennsylvania porthole caboose; 8 curved, 5 straight, UCS, LW transformer.

Comments: While most of the J. C. Penney sets were unassuming, this O Gauge outfit was not. It was almost the best that Lionel had to offer, and at a price 30 percent less than the consumer catalogue's suggested retail price, some feathers were undoubtedly ruffled.

The Virginian FM was reissued by Lionel in 1965 as 2322 to head catalogued outfit 12820. Lionel priced the outfit at $100 in its consumer catalogue, and there was the identical set, priced in the J. C. Penney catalogue at $69.99! This outfit was not outdated inventory; it was new, fresh, top-of-the-line merchandise. Lionel surely "caught some flak" from struggling retailers attempting to obtain the high catalogue price who were faced with taking a return from a customer who had seen the set in the Penney catalogue for considerably less money, or when they lost a sale because a potential customer complained about the glaring price disparity.

The outfit box was a conventional solid white with orange lettering. All of the contents were component boxed, and the set contained a quality LW transformer that alone was separate-sale priced at $20. T. Randazzo Collection. **900 1700**

3718   1965

Contents: 241? steam locomotive; 234W square whistle tender; 6176 black Lehigh Valley hopper; 6142 gondola with canisters; 6473 rodeo car; 3362/3364 operating log car; 6130 Santa Fe work caboose; 260 bumper; 9 curved, 11 straight, 6149, RH manual switch, 147 whistle controller, 1073 transformer.

Comments: The rolling stock for this outfit was the typical mix of O27 Gauge items from the rather bland 1965 product line, but the engine, erroneously shown as a 237 in the catalogue illustration, provokes analysis. The engine included with this set was described as being die

This was another "prototypical" uncatalogued Lionel outfit from the mid-1960s. A steam freight set with an inconsequential Scout-series engine and run-of-the-mill rolling stock from the catalogued line. There are literally dozens of outfits similar to this one. By roster, it hardly deserves mention, but it positively identifies a 1965 J. C. Penney set and a Lionel uncatalogued outfit number. Penney catalogued this set as outfit 3726, but the outfit box also bears the 19437 Lionel uncatalogued number. A. Tolli Collection.

cast; since the 237 has a plastic boiler, however, it certainly could not have been a 237. It was probably a 241, which was new for 1965, and was the engine that was unquestionably included with the 1966 edition of this set, outfit 8287, and with 1965 set 3734.

There are two curious errors in the catalogue illustration of set 3718. First, the tender is shown backwards; second, the two white canisters that belong with

the 6142 gondola are shown riding inside the tool tray of the work caboose.

	VG	LN
	250	450

3726 / 19437   1965

Contents: 237 steam locomotive; 242T streamlined tender; (6402) gray General-type flatcar with cable reels;

VG   LN

6142 gondola with canisters; 6014 white Frisco boxcar; 6059 M St. L SP-type caboose; 12 curved, 3 straight, 6149, 90° crossing, 1010 transformer.

Comments: By roster of content, this set would be difficult to give away; the rolling stock was typical issue from the 1965 product line. What is most informative about the outfit is that it positively identifies a Lionel 19400 series uncatalogued set number. The outfit box was a Type D display style with 1965 graphics which had "19437" rubber stamped on the narrow end of the lid. A. Tolli Collection.   **100   175**

3734 / 19438   **1965**

Contents: 241 steam locomotive; 234W square whistle tender; 6651 olive drab cannon car; 6014 white Frisco boxcar; 6076 black Lehigh Valley hopper; 6465 orange Lionel Lines tank car; 6059 M St. L SP-type caboose; 8 curved, 5 straight, 6149, 147 whistle controller, 1073 transformer.

Comments: Surprise! Surprise! Even though the illustration in the Penney catalogue featured the 237 engine, this outfit actually contained the scarce, un-

VG   LN

catalogued by Lionel, die-cast 241. As an additional bonus, this example of the 241 engine was the even more scarce narrow-stripe variation. The rolling stock, except for the 6651 "Big Bertha" cannon car, was run-of-the-mill. This is the only set in which the 6651 has been verified as a component; it is believed that it was originally issued separately by Lionel as an S & H Green Stamp car. Lionel's decision to include the 6651 in this outfit was undoubtedly a last ditch effort to deplete excess inventory; it does not relate in any manner to the conventional freight roster. M. Sokol Collection.   **450   850**

4782   **1963**

Contents: 238 steam locomotive; 234W square whistle tender; 6822 night crew searchlight car; 6465 orange Lionel Lines tank car; 6414 auto loader; 6476 Lehigh Valley hopper; 6162 gondola with canisters; 6257-100 red SP-type caboose with stack; 8 curved, 3 straight, 6139, 147 whistle controller, 1073 transformer.

Comments: This set appears to be identical to catalogued outfit 11375. The 1963 consumer catalogue lists the suggested retail price at $39.95, but J. C. Penney

Purportedly, the 6651 "Big Bertha" cannon car was issued separately by Lionel as an S & H Green Stamp car. Because of truck and coupler data, the car is dated to late 1963 or early 1964. By 1965 it was "dead" inventory looking for a place to be buried. Lionel found a suitable cemetery—1965 J. C. Penney outfit 3734. P. Michael Collection.

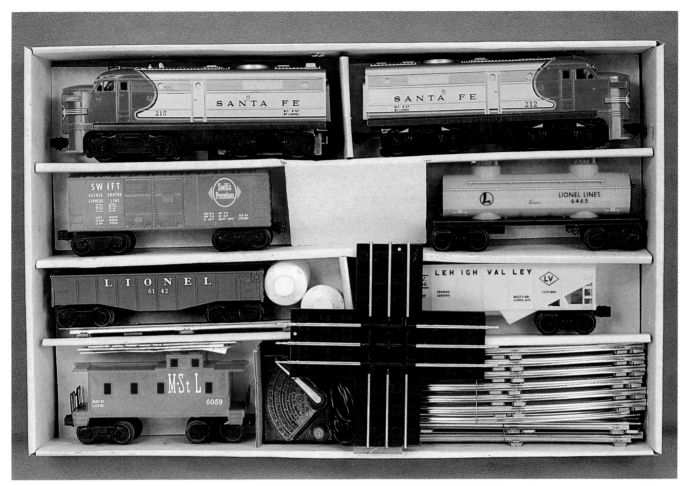

This Santa Fe Alco outfit was featured in the 1966 J. C. Penney catalogue as set 8279. Note that it pairs a 215P (power) unit with a 212T (trailer) unit. The lid of the Type D display-style outfit box was rubber stamped "19506", positively identifying a Lionel set number from the uncatalogued series. What is more interesting about this set is that is was also catalogued by Spiegel in 1966, as their outfit 5260/19507. A. Vincent Collection.

VG   LN

offered the set for $29.98, approximately 25 percent less than Lionel's suggested retail.

The outfit box was probably a tan conventional two-tier type with a combination of boxed and unboxed contents. Truck and coupler types varied, but each item was fitted with one operating coupler. Two items in the set pique collector interest; the -100 SP-type caboose with Type 4 lettering and a die-cast smokestack, and the 6414 auto loader. The 6414 was usually the scarce example that came with the "cheap" autos that had neither wind shields, wheels, nor bumpers.   **600   1000**

4881   1963

Contents: 634 Santa Fe diesel switcher; 3410 flat-car with operating helicopter; (6407) flatcar with rocket; 6014 white Frisco boxcar; 6463 rocket fuel tank car; 6059 red M St. L SP-type caboose; 8 curved, 1 straight, 6139, 1010 transformer.

Comments: This set appears to be identical to

VG   LN

catalogued outfit 11341. J. C. Penney offered the set for $18.88 while the Lionel catalogue had it priced at $25.

The outfit box was probably a Type A display style with the new 1963 graphics. Truck and coupler types varied as they did with most 1963 outfits, but each rolling stock item came with one fixed and one operating coupler. This is an extremely difficult set to obtain in any condition when complete with original parts. The 6407 is one of the rarest and most collectible of all the military/space-related items. The consumer catalogue lists the Frisco boxcar as having a coin slot, but this set usually surfaces with the boxcar having no slot. The 1963 Spiegel catalogue featured a version of this outfit as set 5287.

                                  725   1300

4899   1963

Contents: 237 steam locomotive; 1060T stream-lined tender; 6050 Swift savings bank car; 6465 orange Lionel Lines tank car; (6408) flatcar with pipes; 6162 gondola with canisters; 6119-100 red/gray DL & W work caboose; 8 curved, 1 straight, 6139, 1025 transformer.

VG   LN

Comments: We assume this outfit came with un-boxed contents in a Type A display-style set box with 1963 graphics because it was identical to catalogued outfit 11351. J. C. Penney offered this set for $22.95, which was approximately a 25 percent savings over the listed Lionel catalogue price of $29.95. The rolling stock came with varying types of trucks and couplers, but each component except the tender was fitted with one operating coupler.

125   200

8261   1966

Contents: 237 steam locomotive; 242T streamlined tender; (6408) flatcar with pipes; 6465 orange Lionel Lines tank car; 6050 Swift savings bank car; 6059 M St. L SP-type caboose; 12 curved, 3 straight, 6149, 90° crossing, 1025 transformer.

Comments: The 237 also headed Lionel catalogued outfits in 1963 and 1964, and here it appears again in 1966. One can only assume that Lionel owned inventory on this engine by the ton. Unfortunately, this set was nothing more than a common steam outfit with unexciting rolling stock. Note that the tender has been given 242T nomenclature because it was electrically grounded, necessary because of the inclusion of the 90° crossing.

100   175

8279 / 19506   1966

Contents: 215P/212T Santa Fe Alco AA units; 6050 Swift savings bank car; 6142 gondola with canisters; 6465 orange Lionel Lines tank car; 6176 black Lehigh Valley

VG   LN

hopper; 6059 M St. L SP-type caboose; 12 curved, 7 straight, 6149, 90° crossing, 1073 transformer.

Comments: This outfit came with unboxed contents in a Type D display-style set box with 1965 graphics. The rolling stock was the routine mix of items from the 1965-1966 product line. Interestingly, the contents exactly match Lionel uncatalogued set 19506, and an identical set was catalogued by Spiegel in 1966 as outfit 5260/19507. The 215 Santa Fe Alco unit was not catalogued by Lionel, but it is a known component of several sets from the era. As with the 223 from outfit 0672, it was paired with a 212T dummy A unit. T. Klaassen and A. Vincent Collections.   175   350

8287   1966

Contents: 241 steam locomotive; 234W square whistle tender; 6473 rodeo car; 6176 black Lehigh Valley hopper; 6142 gondola with canisters; 3364 operating log car; 6130 Santa Fe work caboose; 260 bumper; 9 curved, 11 straight, 6149, RH manual switch, 147 whistle controller, 1073 transformer.

Comments: This was a repeat of 1965 outfit 3718; it was given a new number and a price increase from $34.44 to $37.77. The catalogue illustration clearly depicts the steam engine as a 241. The two photographic errors from 1965 were also corrected; the tender was positioned properly (not backward), and the canisters were correctly placed inside the gondola. The uncatalogued die-cast 241 is one of the most prized of the 200 Scout-series engines.   250   450

Firestone

A Train Stop in Ohio

Our knowledge about Firestone sets is so limited that we are reluctant to call this a chapter. But a first step must be taken before others can follow, so let us begin.

Not too many years ago scarcely anyone knew that 11-L-series outfit numbers were attributed to Firestone. Who would think that the Firestone Tire and Rubber Company of Akron, Ohio, would be selling Lionel electric trains through their service centers? But they did.

Besides Lionel trains, Firestone featured products from the Marx line, retailed other toys for both girls and boys, and marketed a Christmas record album each year. Their venture into the realm of toys was definitely a fourth-quarter endeavor, and must have been at least moderately successful, since we can date Lionel merchandise sold through Firestone as early as 1950. We also know that Firestone continued to sell Lionel products into at least the late 1950s, which means they were a Lionel customer for a decade or more.

Upon contacting Firestone, the authors were told by their Public Relations Department that they no longer maintain archives, and unfortunately, there exists no information that would be of any assistance to us in our research.

In addition to Lionel outfits, Firestone also sold individual items. The yellow 2023 Union Pacific Alco AA pair from 1950 has been observed by the authors in a master carton with the number "11-L-129" written on the box in black crayon. We believe that all Lionel outfits sold through Firestone before 1956 were just regular production sets, with Lionel outfit numbers, that were packaged in ordinary Lionel set cartons. The only way to know that a set originated from Firestone is by the presence of either a Firestone price sticker or a handwritten (usually in crayon) Firestone stock number. In 1956, however, Lionel began to stamp outfit boxes at the factory in the 11-L series for Firestone. We believe that most of these post-1955 sets were still the same as the Lionel catalogued outfits, but were numbered differently.

We list only one Firestone set in this chapter. However, we have included a chart with 11-L-series outfit numbers for those sets from Firestone that we can positively identify. Although we are aware of several other Firestone outfits, we cannot list with certainty the contents of those sets; therefore, they are not shown in the chart. Hopefully, with concerned collector input, this chart will grow by leaps and bounds in future editions.

Firestone Outfit Numbers

Firestone Outfit Number	Engine	Year	Firestone Price	Comparable Lionel Number
11-L-19	2245	1954	$69.50	1520W
11-L-40	520	1956	unknown	1542/750
11-L-41	627	1956	unknown	1543/700
11-L-42	2018	1956	unknown	1547S/702
11-L-51	1615	1957	$49.95	X-400
11-L-53	202	1957	$24.95	1569/725
11-L-55	205	1957	$37.50	1575/728
11-L-56	2037	1957	$43.75	1579S/731
11-L-58	204	1957	$50.00	1586/735
11-L-59	2037	1957	$50.00	1583WS/733
11-L-60	2339	1957	$50.00	2275W/815
11-L-62	665	1957	$56.25	2277WS/817
11-L-63	2243	1957	$62.50	2281W/819
11-L-64	2331	1957	$68.75	2285W/821
11-L-256	217	1959	unknown	1615
11-L-259	2329	1959	unknown	2529W

Note: Outfits that can be identified by a comparable Lionel catalogued set number are *not* discussed in this text; please refer to *Volume III* for contents.

11-L-51/X-400   **1957**

Contents: 1615 steam switcher; 1615T slope-back tender; 6014 Baby Ruth or Frisco boxcar; 6424 flatcar with autos; 6025 Gulf tank car; 6017 SP-type caboose; boxed 310 billboard set; 214 girder bridge; 309 yard sign set; 10 curved, 6 straight, 1008 camtrol, pair of manual switches, 1015 transformer.

Comments: This outfit was 1957 Lionel uncatalogued set X-400 that was touted as "SUPER SPE-

                                 VG   **LN**

CIAL / 42 Piece Lionel Freight Set". It was probably available on the open market, but was also featured in a 1957 Firestone brochure with a price of $49.95. The brochure also stated that the items were valued at $62.55 if purchased separately. This set is doubly informative because it identifies both a Firestone stock number in the 11-L series and an uncatalogued Lionel outfit number. J. Algozzini and P. Ambrose observation based upon information furnished by R. Bretch.   **425**   **800**

Observe the Lionel factory-stamped number that appears on the set box; all outfits in the 11-L series came from Firestone. This example, 1956 outfit 11-L-41, was headed by the 627 Lehigh Valley center cab and was a duplicate of catalogued set 1543/700. 1956 was the first year in which Lionel numbered outfit cartons specifically for Firestone. The 6017 caboose included with this set was the scarce example that was stamped only "LIONEL", not "LIONEL LINES", on its sides. V. Bibelot Collection.

General Retailers

WHAT THE REST OF AMERICA HAD TO OFFER

This chapter lists contents and offers comments on all Lionel uncatalogued sets (those that can be positively identified at this time) that were *not* sold through Sears, Montgomery Ward, Spiegel, J. C. Penney, or Firestone. Our entries run the gamut from inconsequential low-end sets to some of the most actively pursued outfits that Lionel ever made, catalogued or otherwise.

The contents of some uncatalogued sets boggles the mind, as do several current values. Some of the miscellany alone, such as the cardstock nuclear submarine station from outfit X714, can cost a week's salary. We have seen an unassembled example sell for $500!

Each and every collector has specific interests as well as a comfort level when it comes to expenditures for toy trains. It has been our observation that uncatalogued sets with unique packaging, accessories, and/or those that featured items not available in catalogued sets arouse collector interest far more than those outfits that were near duplicates of catalogued offerings. Quite often a highly desirable uncatalogued set can be bought for a fraction of its true market value because the seller is unaware of the scarcity of his outfit. Remember that some uncatalogued sets were put into the marketplace with fewer than 200 to 250 outfits available for sale.

Outfit Numbers for Promotional Series Marketed through General Retailers

X 100 Series	1956	3100 Series	1946-47
X 200 Series	1956	10600 Series	1969
X 200 Series (repeat)	1963	11600 Series	1968
X 300 Series	1956-57	19000 Series	1962
X 400 Series	1957	19100 Series	1962
X 500 Series	1957	19200 Series	1963
X 500 NA Series	1960	19300 Series	1964
X 600 Series	1958	19400 Series	1965
X 600 Series (repeat)	1961	19500 Series	1966
X 700 Series	1959	19600 Series	1966-67
X 800 Series	1959-60	19700 Series	1967
X 800 NA Series	1961	19800 Series	1968
1100 Series	1960-61	19900 Series	1969

Note: There are many exceptions to the information above that are not presented in the chart. For example, the Channel Master sets were numbered in the 9700s, and other outfit boxes for unknown retailers have been observed in the 2000 series. Furthermore, many independent retailers assigned their own inventory control numbers. Sears utilized 5900 numbers (1946-51), 9600 numbers (1952-62), 9700 numbers (various years), and 9800 numbers (1964-66). Firestone numbered their outfits in the 11-L series while Sperry and Hutchinson used a series of numbers usually prefaced by "S & H" and/or "6P".

The use of an "X" in outfit numbering was inconsistent. Some sets from the X 100 to X 800 series surface without an X prefix while others from the 19100 to 19900 range occasionally appear with either an X prefix or suffix. At this time we are unable to determine the meaning of "NA" in the X 500 NA and X 800 NA series. On occasion, an outfit number was reused, and then included a suffix such as -100, -500 and -502; when these suffixes appear, the set contents usually differed from what was packaged in the box without a suffix.

VG   LN

149   1956

Contents: 2018 steam locomotive; 6026T square tender; 6014 red Baby Ruth boxcar; 6112 black gondola with canisters; 6025 black Gulf tank car; 6017 SP-type caboose; 8 curved, 3 straight; 6029; 1015 transformer.

Comments: This run-of-the-mill set was quite unusual because the end of the set box was also stamped "Gifts Galore", the name of a small independent retail chain in the Southeast. The outfit box was a single-tier basket weave type, and the set was identical in every respect to Lionel catalogued set 1547S and Firestone uncatalogued outfit 11-L-42, except that a 6025 tank car

was substituted for the 6121 flatcar with pipes in the other two sets. The engine in this outfit, while not in the previously mentioned Firestone or Lionel sets, was component boxed while the other items, with bar-end trucks, were separated and held in place by cardboard dividers. P. Adler Collection.   **175   375**

X-150   1956

Contents: 520 GE box cab electric; 6012 black gondola; 6014 Chun King boxcar; 6017 SP-type caboose; 8 curved, 1 straight; 6029; 1015 transformer.

This is 1956 outfit 149, shown here with a set box specifically stamped for Gifts Galore along with two other outfit boxes. Although the contents of the set are not especially noteworthy, examine the three outfit boxes shown here. The Gifts Galore set was packaged with components nearly identical to those of Lionel catalogued outfit 1547S and Firestone set 11-L-42. The dimensions for the Gifts Galore set box are the same as those used for the 1547S and 11-L-42 boxes. Most uncatalogued outfits of the mid-1950s were surprisingly similar to the catalogued offerings. P. Adler Collection.

As the low number implies, 1956 outfit X-150 was one of the earliest uncatalogued sets, and was the first to include a special promotional car. It contained the scarce and collectible 6014 Chun King boxcar. Except for the substitution of the Chun King boxcar for a 6014 Baby Ruth, this set was identical, even in the dimensions of the outfit carton, to Lionel catalogued set 1542/750. S. Bradley Collection.

	VG	LN

Comments: The outfit box was an undersized basket weave type that was identical except for the number to catalogued set 1542/750, which was also headed by the 520 engine. The components were unboxed and, as with all 1956 items, came with bar-end trucks. The engine was held in place and protected by a uniquely shaped cardboard filler. This is one of the more collectible of the uncatalogued sets as it contained the scarce Chun King boxcar, which was substituted for the Baby Ruth of the catalogued set. One example of this set was reportedly awarded by a Rochester, New York, grocery store as a prize in a bread promotion raffle. S. Bradley and R. Scott Collections. **250 550**

X-400 1957

Contents: 1615 steam switcher. Please refer to Firestone set 11-L-51.

X-444 1957

Contents: 250 steam locomotive; 250T streamlined Pennsylvania tender; 6112 gondola with canisters; 6025 Gulf tank car; 6476 Lehigh Valley hopper; 6024 RCA Whirlpool boxcar; 6017 SP-type caboose; 8 curved, 3 straight, 6029, 1015 transformer.

Comments: The outfit box was a conventional two-tier basket weave type with a paste-on outfit identification label. This is one of the more collectible of the uncatalogued sets as it purportedly contained a special promotional item, namely the 6024 Whirlpool boxcar. The contents, except for the 6024, were commonplace items for 1957 and were packaged in a combination of both boxed and unboxed items.

A contradiction arises because this set has also been reported with a 6464-425, 6424 flatcar with autos, and a red 6121 flatcar with pipes in lieu of the 6112, 6025 and

VG   LN

6476 listed above. We are including this listing only because it may identify another set in which the uncatalogued Whirlpool boxcar appears. The 6024 Whirlpool was also a component of outfit X-589. Additional information requested. A. Vincent and T. Austern Collections.   **150   300**

X-516NA / 6P4803   1960

Contents: 246 steam locomotive; 1130T streamlined tender; 6062 gondola with cable reels; 6825 flatcar with trestle; 6017 SP-type caboose; 8 curved, 2 straight, 1008 camtrol, 1015 transformer.

Comments: The outfit box was a single-tier tan conventional type with boxed components. All boxes had perforated fronts, the norm for 1960. The second number indicates that this set was available through Sperry and Hutchinson, the Chicago-based Green Stamp house. We also have S & H listings for outfits 11331, 19350 and 19350-500.

This set is quite similar to catalogued outfit 1627S, except that it substituted the engine and tender listed above for the 244 and 244T of the catalogued issue. J. Algozzini, M. McFadden and P. Adler Collections.
                                                          150   325

VG   LN

X-526NA   1960

Contents: 246 steam locomotive; 1130T streamlined tender; 6062 gondola with cable reels; 6014-100 Airex boxcar; 6017 SP-type caboose; 12 curved, 4 straight, 1008 camtrol, 90° crossing, 1015 transformer.

Comments: This outfit came in a single-tier tan conventional carton. Though the example reported here did not include any boxes, we assume that each item was component boxed when the set left the factory, based upon our study of similar sets from 1960. The -100 red Airex boxcar was never illustrated in the consumer catalogue, but it did appear in advance catalogues and is a known component of several other promotional sets. G. Ligon Collection.   **125   250**

X-531NA   1960

Contents: 220P/220T Santa Fe Alco AA units; 3419 flatcar with operating helicopter; 6830 flatcar with non-operating submarine; 6650 flatcar with IRBM launcher; 470 missile launch platform with 6470 exploding boxcar; 6017 SP-type caboose; 110 trestle set; 17 curved, 9 straight, 6029, 1015 transformer.

Comments: 1960 offered some exceptionally good uncatalogued outfits and this is one of them. The 220

Although the roster of contents included with this outfit are of minimal collector interest, note that each was component boxed. All items can be readily found at a local train meet, but the outfit box is a rare discovery. Very few sets that can be attributed to Sperry and Hutchinson (S & H), the Chicago-based Green Stamp house, have survived. Cash did not change hands at S & H, only Green Stamp booklets. Because these were often considered to be "free" trains, most sets obtained through S & H were put into the hands of children, not collectors, who treated them with much less than tender loving care. J. Algozzini Collection.

VG   LN

Santa Fe units were the uncatalogued version of the 218 without horn and only a two-position reversing unit. All items came in perforated-front component boxes and were packaged in an oversized generic tan two-tier outfit carton.

Lionel produced the Santa Fe Alco with war bonnet paint scheme under five different numbers. Each time a modification was made to the "guts," the number changed. In our opinion, the 220 ranks just below the 223 in terms of collectibility. L. Harold Collection.   **450**   **900**

X-532NA   1960

Contents: 244 steam locomotive; 244T slope-back tender; 6062 gondola with cable reels; 3376 operating giraffe car; 6465-110 Cities Service tank car; 6017 SP-type caboose; 8 curved, 2 straight, 1008 camtrol; 1015 transformer.

Comments: The outfit box for this set was a yellow background, Type A display style with unboxed components. The rolling stock was commonplace for the year and came with AAR trucks and operating couplers. One example observed had a Macy's retail price sticker. This set has also been reported in Mint condition with a 6343 barrel ramp car instead of the tank car. The 6343 presents a contradiction in dates because it was not catalogued

VG   LN

until 1961. The substitution of cars may have been done at the factory, but more likely it was done at store level a year or more after issue to either replace the tank car, which may have been sold separately, or to exchange it at the request of the purchaser for another item. B. Myles Collection.   **100**   **225**

X-533NA   1960

Contents: 228 Canadian National Alco A unit; 6544 missile firing trail car; 3419 flatcar with operating helicopter; 6844 missile carrying flatcar; 6017 SP-type caboose; track and transformer unknown.

Comments: The outfit box was a 1960 Type A display style with orange and white graphics. This set, though uncatalogued, had a roster of military-related items that were good enough to be included with Super O outfits! The inclusion of the 228 Alco unit leads one to believe that this set was primarily intended for the Canadian market. Reported by D. Bauer.   **300**   **650**

X-544NA   1960

Contents: 246 steam locomotive; 1130T streamlined tender; 6162 gondola with canisters; 6476 red

We wish we could tell you how wonderful this outfit is, but unfortunately, the only thing noteworthy about the set is the outfit box. Although 1960 set X-532NA had the standard mix of regular production Lionel items, it does positively identify the contents of an uncatalogued set, the primary purpose of this book. B. Myles Collection.

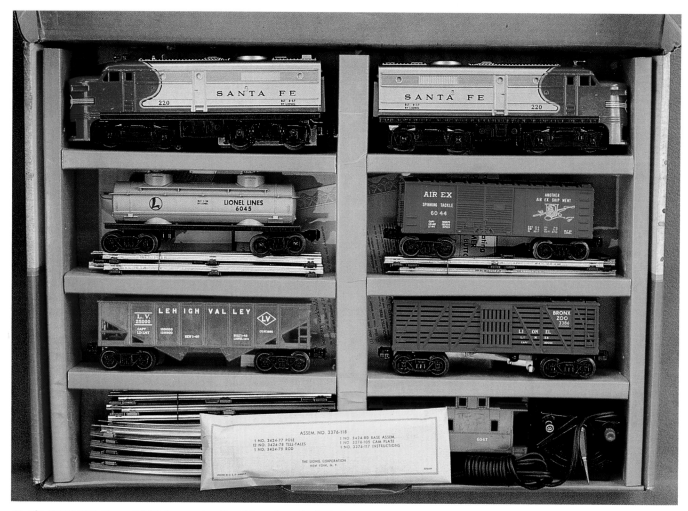

Outfit X-568NA from 1960 is most collectible. It included the scarce uncatalogued 220 Santa Fe Alco units along with some of the more desirable uncatalogued rolling stock items, namely the gray 6045 tank car and the 3386 giraffe car. The long manila envelope (Assem. No. 3376-118) held all of the necessary parts to make the giraffe car operational. The best items included with this outfit, however, were the two packages of 902 elevated trestle set. P. Michael Collection.

No. 902 elevated trestle set is a scarce paper collectible that was included with set X-568NA. The Lionel lion announces the contents of the paper bag. Note that the package contained "10 ELEVATED TRESTLES", but outfit X-568NA actually contained twelve pieces of track! Hence, Lionel included two packages of 902 with set X-568NA to cover the current "shortage" and allow for future expansion as well. P. Michael Collection.

This is the set box for 1960 promotional set X573NA. Something must have gone awry with the promotion of this set because some outfits were relabeled and sold to Channel Master as their set 9745. T. Randazzo Collection.

	VG	LN

Lehigh Valley hopper; 6057 SP-type caboose; 953 Plasticville figure set; 8 curved, 2 straight, 1008 camtrol, 1015 transformer.

Comments: The engine and rolling stock included with this outfit were not at all impressive, but the set included the very collectible 953 Plasticville figure set in a Lionel box. All Plasticville accessories with Lionel boxes are exceptionally scarce, and from a collector's point of view, the 953 has more value than all the other components combined.

Each item in the set came individually boxed; the engine was in a corrugated carton while the other items came in Orange Perforated boxes. The outfit box was a tan conventional two-tier type. T. Randazzo Collection.

125 250

X-550NA   1960

Contents: 228 Canadian National Alco A unit; 3419 flatcar with operating helicopter; 6544 missile firing trail car; 6470 exploding boxcar; 6017 SP-type caboose; 943 exploding ammo dump; 8 curved, 3 straight, 6029, 1015 transformer.

Comments: This was another outfit headed by the uncatalogued 228 Canadian National. It was quite similar in roster to set X-533NA but had all items component boxed and came in a generic tan two-tier outfit carton. The military-related rolling stock was quite im-

pressive for an uncatalogued set and was some of the best Lionel had to offer in 1960. An example of the 6544 with unbroken brakestands is extremely difficult to obtain. Reported by R. Morgan.

325 700

X-556   1957

Contents: 2350 New Haven EP-5; 3424 Wabash brakeman; 6464-425 New Haven boxcar; 6424 flatcar with autos; 6477 miscellaneous car with pipes; 6427 porthole caboose; 8 curved, 7 straight, UCS.

Comments: By definition, this does not qualify as an uncatalogued set because it is identical in content to catalogued O Gauge outfit 2279W/818; it does, however, positively confirm the use of a number in the uncatalogued sequence. The outfit box was the typical basket weave type that was relabeled "X-556"; when the X-556 label was steamed loose by a curious owner, it revealed the number "818", which is the three-digit number that corresponds to 2279W! One can only speculate why this set was numbered as such. Perhaps it was unsold merchandise, offered to the market as a close-out, or it may have been sold at regular price to a secondary retailer and numbered for promotional purposes, rather than the regular numbering sequence for catalogued sets, so as not to antagonize a major retailer in the area. Subterfuge such as this is not uncommon in the manufacturing industry. B. Yeaton Collection.

550 950

	VG	LN

X-568NA   1960

Contents: 220P/220T Santa Fe Alco AA units; 6476 red Lehigh Valley hopper; 6044 Airex boxcar; 6045 gray Lionel Lines tank car; 3386 operating giraffe car; 6047 SP-type caboose; two 902 (cardboard) elevated trestle sets; 8 curved, 4 straight, 1008 camtrol, 1015 transformer.

Comments: The outfit box was a Type A display style with mid-1960s orange-white graphics. This is a very collectible set because the components were some of the more desirable of the uncatalogued items. The 6045 is a scarce and undervalued tank car, and the 3386 is far more collectible than the catalogued 3376. A camtrol was included with this outfit, even though most rolling stock came with fixed coupler, arch bar trucks. This set also included two packages of a unique trestle set that was assembled from die-cut cardboard stock. A. Vincent, C. Hoppa and P. Michael Collections.   **350   750**

X573NA   1960

Contents: 243 steam locomotive; 1130T streamlined tender; 6162 gondola with canisters; 3376 operating giraffe car; 6812 track maintenance car; 3512 fireman and ladder car; 6017 SP-type caboose; 128 animated newsstand; 12 curved, 8 straight, 1008 camtrol, 90° crossing, 1015 transformer.

Comments: The outfit box was an oversized conventional tan type with boxed components. All boxes had perforated fronts, the norm for 1960 production. This was by no means an inexpensive set as evidenced by the inclusion of three "better" cars (3376, 3512 and 6812) from the catalogue roster, and the 128 newsstand, which had a 1960 retail price of $9.95. 1960 was the last year in which the newsstand was catalogued, and its inclusion in this set was a means by which to deplete existing shelf inventory. The promotion of this set must have been unsatisfactory; either orders were canceled or unsold outfits returned to Lionel because some sets were eventually relabeled and sold to Channel Master as outfit 9745. Please refer to 9745 for additional information. I. D. Smith and T. Randazzo Collections.   **400   750**

X-579NA   1960

Contents: 224P/224C U.S. Navy Alco AB units; 6544 missile firing trail car; 3419 flatcar with operating helicopter; 3830 flatcar with operating submarine; 470 missile launch platform with 6470 exploding boxcar; 6017 SP-type caboose; 8 curved, 7 straight, 6029, 1015 transformer.

Comments: This uncatalogued military set is mighty impressive and was as good as anything the Lionel

The uncatalogued 6024 Whirlpool boxcar was a special issue. It was the second such promotional car to be produced by Lionel, the first being the 6014 Chun King from 1956. Outfit X-589 was offered to the employees at the Whirlpool plant in Clyde, Ohio, during the 1957 Christmas season. Although the 204 Santa Fe headed two Lionel catalogued outfits in an AA combination, the Santa Fe was offered here as a single Alco unit. J. Algozzini Collection.

VG LN

catalogue had to offer in 1960. All items came component boxed in a generic tan two-tier outfit carton. There appears to have been an abundance of military-related uncatalogued outfits in 1960. Refer to outfit X-584NA for another set headed by U.S. Navy Alco units. T. Austern Collection.   **425 950**

X-580NA   **1960**

Contents: 1060 steam locomotive; 1060T streamlined tender; 6042 blue gondola with canisters; 6045 Cities Service tank car; 6044 Airex boxcar; 6047 SP-type caboose; 8 curved, 4 straight, 1015 transformer.

Comments: This outfit had all of the characteristics and the usual roster of components for the advance catalogue 1100-series outfits from that same period. All components came with fixed coupler, arch bar trucks, but instead of the unique white background used for advance catalogue set boxes, this outfit came in a relabeled (originally 1609), yellow background, Type A display-style box. The 6045 Cities Service tank car, is very collectible, as are other 6045-series cars; note that it was issued by Lionel with this number to differentiate it from the 6465-110 catalogued version. M. Wisniewski Collection.   **75 200**

X-584NA   **1960**

Contents: 224P/224C U.S. Navy Alco AB units; 6470 exploding boxcar; 3376 operating giraffe car; 3419 flatcar with operating helicopter; 6650 flatcar with IRBM launcher; 6017 SP-type caboose; 8 curved, 3 straight, 6029, 1015 transformer.

Comments: The outfit box was a conventional yellow, two-tier 1959 issue that was relabeled (originally 1626W) and included a Macy's price sticker marked "$27.79". All of the contents were component boxed. At the price listed, this set represented an exceptional value. The engine and rolling stock alone, without track and transformer, had a combined separate-sale price of $50.80, and the giraffe car, new for 1960, was not even offered in a catalogued set that year! Maybe Macy's tried to "make friends" with this set because it was not priced for profitability. Reported by E. Prendeville.
350 700

X-589   **1957**

Contents: 204 Santa Fe Alco A unit; 6024 RCA Whirlpool boxcar; (6111) flatcar with logs; 6112 blue gondola with canisters; 6017 SP-type caboose; 8 curved, 3 straight, 6029, 1015 transformer.

Comments: This outfit came with a combination of boxed and unboxed contents in a single-tier basket weave

set carton. This set is unique because it included a powered Alco A unit *without* the matching dummy. Because it included the uncatalogued Whirlpool boxcar, this outfit is routinely referred to as the "Whirlpool" set. All components came with AAR trucks with rounded axle ends, which was indicative of the style used during 1957.

It has been reported that this set was offered to the employees who were working at the Whirlpool plant in Clyde, Ohio, during Christmas of 1957. Since there were also Whirlpool plants in St. Joseph, Michigan, and Finley, Ohio, it is possible that this set was offered to employees at those places as well. R. Thomas and J. Algozzini Collections.   **250 500**

X600   **1961**

Contents: 246 steam locomotive; 1060T or 1130T streamlined tender; (6406) gray General-type flatcar with gray-bumpered auto; 6042 blue gondola with canisters; 6076 red Lehigh Valley hopper; 6047 SP-type caboose; 8 curved, 2 straight, 1016 transformer.

Comments: This set was part of a special Quaker Oats promotion. The purchaser mailed two Quaker Oats or Mother's Oats box tops and $11.95 to the Quaker Oats company, which then sent the set directly to the customer. The outfit box was a conventional tan two-tier type with unboxed components. The automobile was usually yellow, but this set has also been reported with a black hopper and maroon flatcar, which is plausible. All cars have arch bar trucks and fixed couplers. Lionel informed its service stations about this set and reported that the buyers of this set "are asking where to buy more track and accessories to add to this set. Because of the many thousands of Quaker Oats sets being shipped across the country, you should be selling quite a bit of track and accessories to these new Lionel customers." Lionel went on to say that "if by chance any of the parts of the set have arrived damaged through the mail to these customers, we are giving them the choice of returning the damaged merchandise to us at the factory or visiting you to have the parts repaired or replaced under our normal guarantee." S. Bradley and J. Amanda Collections. **200 450**

X-610NAA   **1958**

Contents: 248 steam locomotive; 1130T streamlined tender; 6014 red Bosco boxcar; (6121) flatcar with pipes; 6476 red Lehigh Valley hopper; (6111) flatcar with logs; 6112 black gondola with canisters; 6017 SP-type caboose; boxed 310 billboard set; 957 Plasticville farm building and animal set; 14 curved, 3 straight, 2 half-curve, 45° crossing, UCS, 1015 transformer.

Comments: The outfit box was a slightly oversized basket weave type with boxed components. All of the rolling stock came with early AAR trucks and a combination of regular and rounded-end axles. Pay particular attention to the NAA suffix; instead of the customary O27

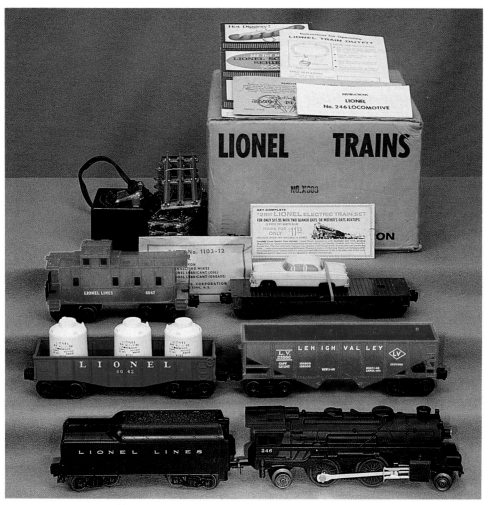

Outfit X600 from 1961 is known as the Quaker Oats set. Except for the yellow automobile, the other contents are deemed inconsequential. This set does, however, have an interesting background. The purchaser mailed two Quaker Oats or Mother's Oats box tops and $11.95 to the Quaker Oats company, which then sent the set directly to the customer via parcel post. Observe the original coupon offer sheet that is propped against the set carton. S. Bradley Collection.

	VG	LN

track, this set came with O Gauge track, and is one of the first known to include a Plasticville accessory (see also X-619). The 248 engine with plastic boiler was the first uncatalogued example in the 200 Scout series. The 6111 stamped-steel flatcar reported with the T. Michels Collection was the scarce wine color while the other components were common 1958 production items. T. Vittorio and T. Michels Collections. **300 600**

X617   1958

Contents: 210P/210T Texas Special Alco AA units?; 6014 Frisco or Bosco boxcar?; 6112 gondola with canisters?; _____?; 6017 SP-type caboose?; 110 trestle set; 12 curved, 7 straight, 6029, 90˚ crossing, 1053 transformer.

Comments: The question marks behind the components listed above indicate that we are not completely

certain that they are correct; one rolling stock item (shown as _____?) is a complete mystery. The Texas Special units, even though offered in only one catalogued set, are quite common. We presume that other contents were nothing more than average 1958 items, but the outfit box was spectacular (refer to photograph on page 81). It was a unique die-cut flat pack with a speckled filler and a cardboard sleeve used as a cover, and it was specially marked for Gifts Galore! Of further interest, it also came with a cardboard easel-type display stand. The set carton closely resembles that which was later used in 1960 for the Halloween General. J. Algozzini Collection.

400 1000

X-619   1958

Contents: 210P/210T Texas Special Alco AA units; 6801 flatcar with boat; 6424 flatcar with autos; 6014

Even with a consist of regular production rolling stock, outfit X-610NAA is most intriguing. The 248 engine with plastic boiler was the first uncatalogued example in the 200 Scout series. This outfit is also the only example reported to have an NAA suffix. We assume that Lionel used "NAA" to indicate O Gauge track, and "NA" for O27 Gauge track. This outfit also contained a boxed 310 billboard set and a 957 Plasticville Farm Building & Animal Set. Plasticville accessories in Lionel packaging are exceptionally scarce. Note the mixture of Classic Lionel boxes; both Late and Bold Classic types were used, the norm for 1958. T. Vittorio Collection.

	VG	LN

orange Bosco boxcar; 6465 gray Gulf tank car; 6112 blue gondola with canisters; 6017 SP-type caboose; 110 trestle set; 145 gateman; boxed 310 billboard set; 966 Plasticville firehouse set; 12 curved, 13 straight, 6029, 1053 transformer.

Comments: If the components had not been printed on the end of the box, the roster of contents would strain one's credulity. The outfit carton was an oversized basket weave type with all items individually boxed. All the rolling stock came with early AAR trucks, and this outfit was identical to the catalogued set 1599 except for the additional track and the accessories. The 45-piece Plasticville firehouse set in a box with Lionel graphics is exceptionally scarce and the most valued component of the set. P. Ambrose Collection.   **350   700**

X640   **1961**

Contents: 233 steam locomotive; 1130T streamlined tender; 6445 Fort Knox car; 3370 sheriff and outlaw car; 6361 timber transport car; 6519 Allis Chalmers car; 6017 SP-type caboose; 5 billboards, 12 curved, 4 straight, 90° crossing, 1008 camtrol, 1025 transformer.

Comments: This outfit came in a solid orange conventional two-tier box with individually boxed components. The new-issue 233 engine came in a corrugated carton while the other new-issue 6445 and 3370 were packaged in Orange Picture boxes; the remainder of the carryover rolling stock came in Orange Perforated boxes. This was *not* a low-end set as evidenced by the higher quality rolling stock that was offered; the 6445 and 3370

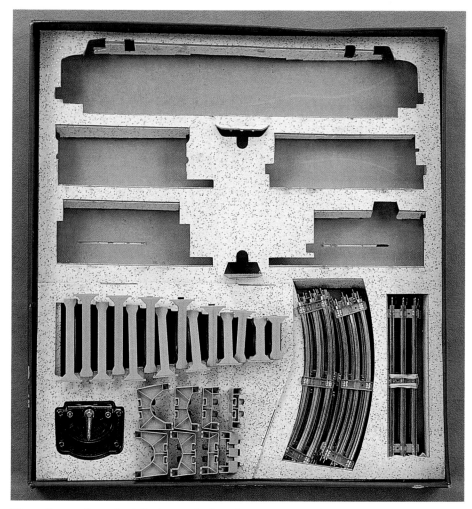

Have the authors lost their minds by showing a nearly empty box? Quite the contrary; even though the box is almost empty, it is a collector's dream. Outfit X617 was a special uncatalogued set for Gifts Galore. The box is shown in this manner because we are not absolutely sure of the correct roster; it was purchased without contents just for the box itself. Facsimiles of this flat-pack style of box with "speckled" die-cut filler were also used for a 219 Missouri Pacific Alco set from 1959 (number unknown) and for the 1960 Halloween General set (number also unknown). J. Algozzini Collection.

	VG	LN

sold for $5.95 and $7.95 respectively. The 6519 was no doubt "dead" inventory; it was offered in one 1961 catalogued set, but not listed as available for separate sale.

To our good fortune, we have been able to locate a listing of this outfit in a special-issue catalogue from an unknown retailer. It was featured in color across two pages as set "T18-6", and sold for $29.88. Reported by D. Bauer. **200 450**

X-643 1958

Contents: 212 U.S.M.C. Alco A unit; 6803, 6804, and 6809 flatcars with military units; 6807 flatcar with

	VG	LN

military DKW; 6175 red flatcar with rocket; 6017-85 gray SP-type caboose; pair of manual switches; 253 block signal; track and transformer unknown.

Comments: This uncatalogued military outfit was a prize awarded by Seabrook Farms (located near Bridgeton, New Jersey), a wholesale supplier for grocery and convenience stores, to those merchants who ordered a certain dollar amount of Seabrook Farm products. It was an impressive set, and every item included is now in collector demand. The outfit carton was a two-tier basket weave type that was relabeled "X-643", and all items were component boxed. The 6800-series military units were made for Lionel by Pyro, and they are all extremely fragile. J. Algozzini Collection. **700 1600**

This is the outer carton for Gifts Galore promotion set X617. Most fortunately for collectors and researchers, it is marked with an outfit number. We only wish the same were so for the Halloween General set. J. Algozzini Collection.

If the components of 1958 outfit X-619 were not printed on the end of the set box, one would most likely not believe the roster of contents. Lionel had the foresight in 1958 to list the contents of a promotional set on the carton, but shortly thereafter, did a complete about-face and did not routinely state contents of uncatalogued sets again until 1966! P. Ambrose Collection.

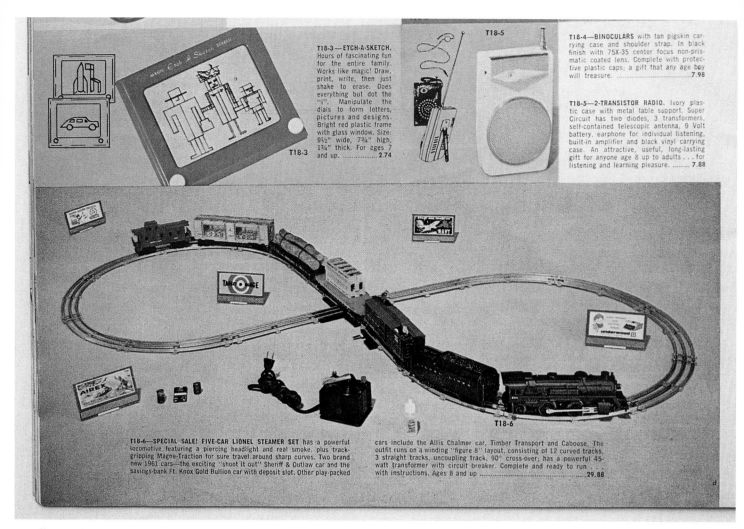

T18-3—ETCH-A-SKETCH. Hours of fascinating fun for the entire family. Works like magic! Draw, print, write, then just shake to erase. Does everything but dot the "i". Manipulate the dials to form letters, pictures and designs. Bright red plastic frame with glass window. Size: 9½" wide, 7¾" high, 1¾" thick. For ages 7 and up. 2.74

T18-4—BINOCULARS with tan pigskin carrying case and shoulder strap. In black finish with 75X-35 center focus non-prismatic coated lens. Complete with protective plastic caps; a gift that any age boy will treasure. 7.98

T18-5—2-TRANSISTOR RADIO. Ivory plastic case with metal table support. Super Circuit has two diodes, 3 transformers, self-contained telescopic antenna, 9 Volt battery, earphone for individual listening, built-in amplifier and black vinyl carrying case. An attractive, useful, long-lasting gift for anyone age 8 up to adults . . . for listening and learning pleasure. 7.88

T18-6—SPECIAL SALE! FIVE-CAR LIONEL STEAMER SET has a powerful locomotive featuring a piercing headlight and real smoke, plus track-gripping Magne-Traction for sure travel around sharp curves. Two brand new 1961 cars—the exciting "shoot it out" Sheriff & Outlaw car and the savings-bank Ft. Knox Gold Bullion car with deposit slot. Other play-packed cars include the Allis Chalmer car, Timber Transport and Caboose. The outfit runs on a winding "figure 8" layout, consisting of 12 curved tracks, 3 straight tracks, uncoupling track, 90° cross-over; has a powerful 45-watt transformer with circuit breaker. Complete and ready to run . . . with instructions. Ages 8 and up 29.88

Small miracles sometimes do happen. In our search for material for this book, we uncovered this marvelous picture of a Lionel train set featured in an unusual retail catalogue. Most disappointingly, we could not locate any paperwork to tell us the name of the merchant. This train set was listed as "T18-6", a number not similar to other Lionel reference numbers. However, as we examined our listings, we were elated to discover an exact match to outfit X640. Greenberg Archives.

VG   LN

X-646   1958

Contents: 212P/212T U.S.M.C. Alco AA units; 6803 flatcar with military units; 6807 flatcar with military DKW; 6809 flatcar with military units; 6017-50 U.S.M.C. SP-type caboose; track and transformer unknown.

Comments: This is one of the "best" of the uncatalogued sets because it contained the rare 212T dummy A unit with an *open pilot* and front coupler. Specific mention of this dummy A unit is made in the *Lionel Service Manual*. All items were component boxed; the engines were packaged in 1958-type standard corrugated cartons with protective coupler rings and the remainder in Classic boxes. Two different outfit boxes have been observed. The first box was a conventional basket weave type with "X 646" printed on one end while the other was a relabeled Super O set box (originally

2526W). Both boxes were oversized to accommodate the components, leading one to assume that the outfit may have contained some accessories. L. Harold Collection.

900   2000

X-654   1961

Contents: 1065 Union Pacific Alco A unit; 6630 IRBM launcher; 6480 exploding boxcar; 3409 flatcar with operating helicopter; 6042 blue gondola with canisters; (6120) yellow unstamped work caboose; track and transformer unknown.

Comments: The outfit box was a Type A display style with deep red print that was common to low-end sets in 1961. The components were the same as those in

This impressive military outfit is 1958 set X-643. It was given as a prize to merchants who ordered a certain amount from Seabrook Farms, a wholesale supplier to grocery and convenience stores. In addition to a very collectible roster of military cars, this set also included the somewhat scarce gray SP-type caboose with black Lionel Lines lettering and a 253 block signal. Note that the correct box for the caboose is a Bold Classic type numbered "6017-85". J. Algozzini Collection.

	VG	LN

advanced catalogue set 1125 except for the addition of two extra cars, the 6042 and 3409, which were also components of 1961 advance catalogue sets 1123 and 1124 respectively. Aside from the 6042 gondola, the other components are quite desirable in the collector market, making this one of the better uncatalogued sets. R. Ward Collection.

250 500

X-714 (multiple use of number) 1959

Contents: 602 Seaboard diesel switcher; 6464-375 Central of Georgia boxcar; 6818 flatcar with transformer; 6476 red Lehigh Valley hopper; 6112 blue gondola with canisters; 6017 SP-type caboose; 128 animated newsstand; 12 curved, 4 straight, 1008 camtrol, 90° crossing, 1015 transformer.

Comments: This was the second set for which we have a listing that originated from Seabrook Farms; the other was outfit X-643. All items were component boxed, and because of the generic tan set carton and the outfit number, this set is dated to 1959, even though some of the components, such as the Seaboard switcher and Central of Georgia boxcar, date to 1957 production. This outfit was given as a prize to vendors who ordered a certain dollar amount of Seabrook Farm products. Most generic tan outfit cartons were stamped with black print, but this example was printed in blue. J. Algozzini Collection.

450 850

X714 (multiple use of number) 1961

Contents: 45 U.S. Marines mobile missile launcher; 3830 flatcar with operating submarine; 6530 firefighting instruction car; 3519 satellite car; 3535 security caboose; 943 ammo dump; cardstock atomic submarine base; 16 curved, 4 straight, 1008 camtrol, 45° crossing, 1043 transformer.

Comments: This was a special outfit with a roster of premium cars that was packaged for Masters, a jobber and independent retailer, with locations in New York and Paramus, New Jersey. It reused an outfit number that had previously been assigned to a Seabrook Farm set in 1959. The set carton was a single-tier plain tan type measuring 18⅜ x 22 x 5¼ inches that included individually boxed components, and one of the rarest accessories ever included with a Lionel outfit, the nuclear submarine base.

A newspaper ad dated November 20, 1961, stated the suggested list price at $73.10 while highlighting the Masters' price as "$27.88 complete". The ad also stated "Only 400 sets, 1 per customer. No dealers!"

Examination of the set reveals a few oddities. The transformer case was ivory with a gold handle and came packaged in a Girls' Set transformer box (originally issued in 1957), numbered "1043-500", but the electrical cord and screws for attaching the case were black! To keep the cost low, Lionel included only a camtrol with this O27 Gauge

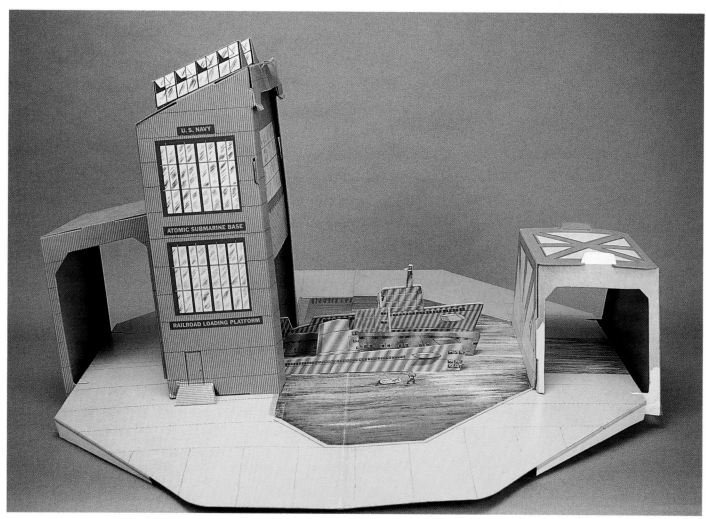

Pictured above is an assembled cardstock atomic submarine base. It is one of the rarest accessories ever included in a Lionel outfit. The track layout plan allowed for the submarine base to be positioned at the inside of a pretzel-shaped loop. Note that the assembled station does not lie flat; the base was designed to have a slight grade. Observe the atomic submarines ready for duty and defense of our shores. By the consist of set X714, we assume that the 3830 flatcar was either delivering a sub to be launched, or picking one up for rail transportation to another port. How thoughtful of Lionel to include a 6530 firefighting instruction car in this set, as if water would do any good in case of a nuclear accident! Too bad the 6805 atomic energy disposal car was not available; it had been out of stock for two years. Can you imagine the repercussions a manufacturer would face today if he tried to promote and sell a train that transported nuclear material? The media would chastise any company foolish enough to try. A. Stewart Collection.

	VG	LN

outfit. The mobile missile launcher was made operational through the use of an OTC contactor and a no. 90 controller. A. Stewart Collection. **1000 2200**

X-802 1960

Contents: 218P/218T Santa Fe Alco AA units; 6464-475 Boston and Maine boxcar; 6519 Allis Chalmers car; 6175 flatcar with rocket; 6820 flatcar with helicopter; 6517 bay window caboose; track unknown, 1053 transformer.

Comments: This outfit came in a generic tan conventional, two-tier set carton that was relabeled "X-802"; each individual item was component boxed. The caboose was carryover merchandise dated to 1957 while the engine and other rolling stock were standard production items for 1960. Of particular interest is the 6820; instead of the catalogued version of the helicopter with "Little John" missiles, this example was reported with a red HO Gauge helicopter that usually came with the 3619 helicopter reconnaissance car. J. Turner Collection as reported in the Summer 1991 edition of the *Atlantic Division Express.* **325 675**

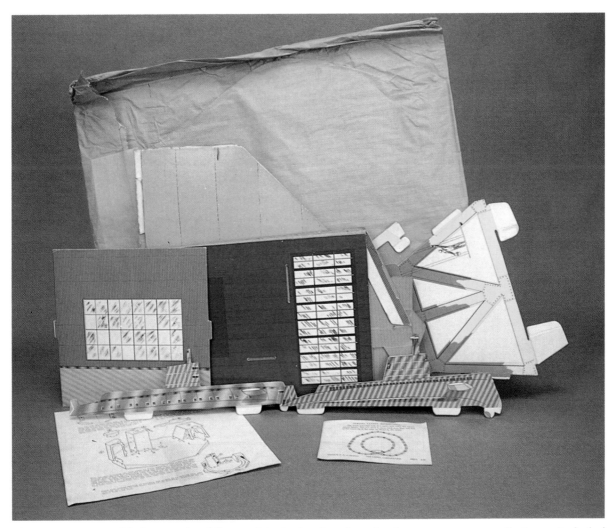

This is an unassembled example of the cardstock atomic submarine base, an accessory that was included with outfit X714 and at least one other set from the early 1960s. It was packaged in a plain brown bag and placed flat inside the outfit carton. Note the pretzel-shaped track plan diagramed on the instruction sheet that is shown in the foreground on the right. A. Stewart Collection.

	VG	LN

X-821NA — 1961

Contents: 243 steam locomotive; 1130T streamlined tender; 6343 barrel ramp car; 6062 gondola with cable reels; 3362 helium tank unloading car; 6057-50 orange SP-type caboose; 8 curved, 8 straight, 1008 camtrol, 1025 transformer.

Comments: This outfit consisted of regular production Lionel items from the catalogued line. The 3362 and 6343 were two new-for-1961 items while the 243 engine was carry-forward inventory from 1960. The set came packaged without component boxes in a generic tan outfit carton. D. Cirillo Collection. **125   250**

DX 837 — 1959

Contents: 246 steam locomotive; 1130T stream-lined tender; 6162 gondola with canisters; 6014-150 W I X boxcar; 6057 SP-type caboose; boxed 310 billboard set; folded 950 railroad map; uncut sheet of 12 Lionel collector cards; 8 curved, 2 straight, 1008 camtrol, 1016 transformer.

Comments: The outfit box (leftover from 1958) was a conventional two-tier basket weave type with boxed components. The outfit number was not printed directly on the box but was instead rubber stamped in black on a special strip of sealing tape. The engine came in a corrugated carton while the other items came in Orange Perforated boxes. This is the only reported set of which the W I X boxcar was a component, and it was evidently commissioned by the W I X Corporation of Gastonia, North Carolina. The boxcar is scarce, and especially so with the proper component box that has a "-150" suffix.

Study this plate closely; outfit DX837 from 1959 has some fascinating contents. Because of the 6014 WIX boxcar, we assume this set must have been somehow affiliated with the WIX Corporation of Gastonia, North Carolina. Note that the factory-correct component box for the WIX boxcar has a -150 suffix. The outfit also contained a folded 950 railroad map and an uncut sheet of twelve Lionel collector cards. Lionel utilized an outdated 1956-1958-era basket weave set carton to package this outfit, and simply rubber stamped the set number over a strip of sealing tape. M. Sokol Collection.

	VG	LN

The box for the 6057 caboose is also scarce and more valuable than the item itself. M. Sokol Collection.

	VG	LN
	400	825

X-875   **1960**

Contents: 246 steam locomotive; 1130T streamlined tender; 6014-100 Airex boxcar; 6476 red Lehigh Valley hopper; 6465 black Lionel Lines tank car; 6017 SP-type caboose; 8 curved, 2 straight, 1008 camtrol, 1016 transformer.

Comments: The outfit box was a conventional tan two-tier generic type. Aside from the fact that this set was headed by the common 246 engine, it is intriguing because

all of the items came component boxed. The engine came in the usual corrugated carton while the other components came in Orange Perforated boxes. The -100 red Airex was uncatalogued by Lionel but surfaces in several uncatalogued sets. Of special interest is the tank car; it came in a box with a "-85" suffix, an exceptionally scarce box. R. Stepan Collection.

	VG	LN
	150	300

1115   **1960**

Contents: 227P Canadian National Alco A unit; 6044 Airex boxcar; 6045 gray Lionel Lines tank car; 6042 blue gondola with canisters; 6047 SP-type caboose; 8 curved, 2 straight, 1026 transformer.

Outfit 1115 was quite similar to 1959 Lionel advance catalogue set 1105. The freight roster was identical but the 227 Canadian National Alco A unit replaced the 1055 Texas Special in outfit 1115. This set was undoubtedly aimed at the Canadian train enthusiast, and is exceptionally scarce in general and more so in the United States. It is very difficult to obtain sets packaged in this manner with a full complement of cardboard dividers. R. Corruthers Collection.

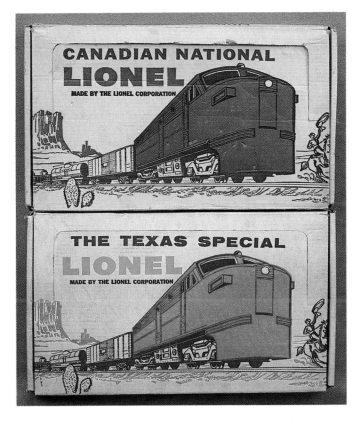

Notice both the similarities and striking differences between these two outfit boxes. The outfit box on the top for set 1115 had the detail printed in green and replaced the Texas Special road name with Canadian National. The bottom example was introduced in 1959 with advance catalogue set 1105; it was utilized again in 1960 for advance catalogue set 1107. R. Corruthers Collection.

VG LN

Comments: This outfit came in a unique white background Type A display-style set box that was similar to that used for the 1055 Texas Special advance catalogue sets of 1959 and 1960. Outfit box 1115 had the detail printed in *green*, rather than red, to match the green paint scheme of the engine. Because of the Canadian National road name, the set was undoubtedly aimed at the Canadian market. The components came with fixed coupler, arch bar trucks, and were the standard, advance catalogue items for the period. The 227 is a more valued collector piece than the similar 228, and the 6045 tank car is both scarce and undervalued. Of interest is the fact that the number "1115" had been previously used by Lionel for a catalogued set in 1949. R. Corruthers Collection.

275 575

1119   1960-1961

Contents: 246 steam locomotive; 1060T streamlined tender; 6042 blue gondola with canisters; 6076 red Lehigh Valley hopper; 6047 SP-type caboose; 8 curved, 2 straight, 1015 transformer.

Comments: The outfit box was a Type A display style with white background that was identical to the box used for advance catalogue set 1109 (Refer to *Volume III* for color photograph). The components all came with fixed coupler, arch bar trucks, and were some of the standard advance catalogue items for the period. Lionel previously used the 1119 outfit number for a catalogued set in 1951-1952. Note that this number falls in between 1960 advance catalogue set numbers 1107 and 1109, and 1961 advance catalogue set numbers 1123, 1124 and 1125. One wonders if there are other outfits, aside from 1115, numbered between 1109 and 1123. Reported by R. Morgan.

100 225

2058   1965

Contents: 242 steam locomotive; 1062T slope-back tender; 638-2361 Van Camp boxcar; 6142 green gondola with canisters; 6176 yellow Lehigh Valley hopper; 6059

red M St. L SP-type caboose; Lionel engineer's cap; 12 curved, 3 straight, 6149, 90° crossing, 1025 transformer.

Comments: This was indeed a strange outfit number, but it was rubber stamped, along with the contents, on the end of a 1965 Type D display-style box. What is most puzzling is the absence of any other number on the box. Note that this set included a Lionel engineer's cap! Most of the contents are inconsequential and of no collector value, but the Van Camp boxcar was the scarce Type 3 example with a coin slot. L. Harold Collection.

150 300

3103W   1946

Contents: 224 steam locomotive; 2466W early coal tender; 2452X gondola; 2454 Baby Ruth boxcar; 3559 coal dump car; 2457 red tinplate caboose; 8 curved, 3 straight, RCS, 1042 transformer.

Comments: This was the first uncatalogued set to appear in the postwar era. It was advertised as available through Madison Hardware on the inside back cover of the October 1946 issue of *Model Builder* magazine. The set was listed at $49.95 and came in a 1945 box (part number 463W-2) with paste-on identification label numbered "3103W". All items were component boxed in 1946 editions of the Art Deco box that did not have the Toy Manufacturer's Association logo. Note that this was an O Gauge set that included a transformer.

The 224 engine had a rounded cab floor and a short drawbar. The tender and rolling stock were also typical 1946 production items. The set box is truly rare, but the contents, if separated from the set, are of minimal collector interest. R. Swanson Collection.

250 500

9745(A)   1960

Contents: 243 steam locomotive; 1130T streamlined tender; 6162 gondola with canisters; 3376 operating

The outfit number of this 1965 set is unique; 2058 is an obvious anomaly, and we cannot even venture a guess as to why a set was numbered as such. The 242 steam engine and rolling stock that came with this outfit are insignificant, but the second line of print in the rubber-stamped legend states "ENGINEER'S CAP". This cap was often illustrated in Lionel's promotional literature and is mentioned as early as 1952, but by 1965 we assume that Lionel was trying to reduce their on-hand position; what better way to do so than through a promotional set? L. Harold Collection.

There were four variations of Channel Master sets that were all numbered "9745"! One wonders how many collectors were aware of that fact. This set was one of the early issues from 1960 and contained the 128 animated newsstand and the premium 3512 fireman and ladder car. For more detail, refer to the comments under outfits X573 NA and 9745(A). J. Algozzini Collection.

	VG	LN

giraffe car; 6812 track maintenance car; 3512 fireman and ladder car; 6017 SP-type caboose; 128 animated newsstand; 12 curved, 8 straight, 1008 camtrol, 90° crossing, 1015 transformer.

Comments: This set was identical to outfit X573 NA except that it also included a large Channel Master sticker and a separate sticker marked "promotion no. 9745 / no. X-573 NA" pasted to one end of the box. Another example included a large white sticker on the side of the carton marked "CHANNEL MASTER / promotion no. 9745". R. Hall and J. Algozzini Collections.   **425   800**

9745(B)   **1960**

Comments: This set was similar to outfits X573 NA and 9745(A), except that a 175 rocket launcher was

	VG	LN

substituted for the 128 animated newsstand, and it included a special Channel Master billboard along with a dark green frame. This outfit box had slightly different dimensions than 9745(A). It also had the Channel Master sticker pasted to one end, but shows no evidence of the X573 NA number. Could it be that Channel Master ordered more outfits than Lionel was able to provide as unsold X573 NA sets and had to assemble some additional outfits to complete the order? The 175 rocket launcher was a poor-selling accessory and an ideal item to offer in a promotional set. It appears that Lionel started depleting shelf inventory on the rocket launcher after inventory on the 128 was exhausted. This action definitely cost Lionel money, and they "took one on the chin" as the 175 was retail priced $10 higher than the animated newsstand! V. Bibelot Collection.   **500   1100**

This was the third variation of the Channel Master set that is listed as 9745(C). All were similar, but each was unique in its own right. Note the unique Channel Master billboard that sits atop the box for the 175 rocket launcher; it was not included with outfits that were relabeled from set X573 NA. The rocket launcher, with a separate-sale price of $19.95, was an expensive accessory to be included as a component of a promotional set. Did Channel Master sets sell well enough to warrant four variations? Probably not; we assume that each set was packaged in limited quantities. E. Dougherty Collection.

	VG	LN

9745(C)   1960

Contents: 243 steam locomotive; 1130T stream-lined tender; 3376 operating giraffe car; 6162 gondola with canisters; 6476 red Lehigh Valley hopper; 6812 track maintenance car; 6057 SP-type caboose; 175 rocket launcher; special Channel Master billboard with dark green frame; 12 curved, 8 straight, 1008 camtrol, 90° crossing, 1015 transformer.

Comments: This set was the third variation of outfit 9745. A tan sticker marked "CHANNEL MASTER / promotion no. 9745" was affixed to one end of the set carton. Some changes in rolling stock were made with this outfit; the caboose became a 6057, and the 3512 was replaced by a 6476 hopper car, probably to offset the

additional cost incurred by the inclusion of the rocket launcher. E. Dougherty Collection.   **475**   **1000**

9745(D)   1960

Contents: 243 steam locomotive; 243W square whistle tender; 3376 operating giraffe car; 6162 gondola with canisters; 6476 red Lehigh Valley hopper; 6057 SP-type caboose; 175 rocket launcher; special Channel Master billboard with dark green frame; 12 curved, 8 straight, 1008 camtrol, 90° crossing, 147 whistle controller, 1015 transformer.

Comments: This was the fourth variation of Channel Master promotional outfit 9745. The contents differed

Outfit 10613 SF is very unassuming, yet it provides some fascinating details about the "goings-on" at the Lionel factory in 1969. The engine was unnumbered, the rolling stock was as low end as possible, and the outfit box (origin Hillside, New Jersey) was numbered totally out of sequence and no longer proclaimed "MANUFACTURED and GUARANTEED BY THE LIONEL CORPORATION". Note that Lionel included two red canisters in this set, probably because they had thousands of them in inventory. L. Vasilion Collection.

	VG	LN

slightly from 9745(C). Notice that although this set had one less rolling stock item (the 6812 was deleted), it did include a whistle tender. Also of interest is this particular outfit box. Its dimensions were slightly different from other boxes, and the Channel Master name and outfit number were type stamped directly on the box. Again, all of the contents were component boxed. Lionel did not include as a set component the 6175 flatcar with rocket, which was the usual (though not essential) complement to the 175 rocket launcher. Please refer to outfit X573 NA for additional information. B. Myles observation.

475   1000

10613 SF   1969

Contents: (1061) unstamped steam locomotive; 1062T streamlined tender; (6402) gray General-type flatcar with cable reels; (6476) gray unstamped hopper; 6167 SP-type caboose; two canisters; 8 curved, 2 straight, 1025 transformer.

Comments: A bland outfit such as this happens to provide some amazing details about what was going on at the Lionel factory in 1969. The outfit box was a plain tan conventional two-tier type that was numbered out of sequence. For no apparent reason, Lionel included two red canisters with this outfit. The theme appears to have been "Anything Goes" when it came to packaging sets.

VG   LN

This 1061 engine was completely unstamped; whether it was a new molding or a cab already in inventory, Lionel did not deem it necessary to number the engine of this promotional set! The tender in this outfit is referred to as "1062" because it was electrically grounded, and the unstamped gray hopper is given 6476 nomenclature because it had operating couplers at both ends. Note that this set did not even include an uncoupling section! It is likely that the hopper shells were unstamped leftovers from a special 493-piece order assembled for the 1969 TTOS Convention held in Los Angles. The special-request gray TTOS hopper was heat stamped in blue lettering; whatever unstamped units remained from the production run were utilized as set components. L. Vasilion Collection.   **100   250**

10653 SF   1969

Contents: 1065 Union Pacific Alco A unit; (6042) green unstamped gondola with canisters; (6402) gray General-type flatcar with cable reels; 6167 SP-type caboose; 8 curved, 2 straight, 1026 transformer.

Comments: This is the second outfit that we report in the "strangely" numbered five-digit series that begins with a "10". The set carton was also a generic tan conventional two-tier type. What is utterly amazing is that Lionel headed this outfit with the 1065 Union Pacific that debuted in 1961 advance catalogue set 1125! Apparently management cleaned out a parts bin and distributed this eight-year-old replacement cab in this outfit. P. Ambrose Collection.   **100   250**

10663 SF   1969

Contents: 1062 steam locomotive; 1060T streamlined tender; 6014-85 orange Frisco boxcar; (6402) gray General-type flatcar with boat; 6059 brown M St. L SP-type caboose; 12 curved, 4 straight, 90° crossing, 1026 transformer.

Comments: Here is the third outfit that we report in the 10600 series that is dated to 1969. Though the contents are inconsequential, we are utterly fascinated by the outfit number. Could all 10600-series outfits have been numbered as such for a specific retailer? R. Okun Collection.   **100   225**

11331 / 6P-4810   1963

Contents: 242 steam locomotive; 1060T streamlined tender; 6473 rodeo car; 6476 red Lehigh Valley hopper; 6142 gondola with canisters; 6059 red M St. L SP-type caboose; 8 curved, 1 straight, 6139; 1010 transformer.

Comments: Outfit 11331 was a Lionel *catalogued* set that came in a Type A display-style box; but it was also available through S & H, the Green Stamp house. This

VG   LN

example had both the Lionel set number and "6P-4810" printed on the lid off the outfit carton. It is listed in this reference only because it identifies an S & H set number. J. Algozzini observation.   **125   225**

11540-500   1966

Contents: 239 steam locomotive; 242T streamlined tender; 6473 rodeo car; 6176 black Lehigh Valley hopper; 6465 orange Lionel Lines tank car; 6162 gondola with canisters; 6119-100 red/gray DL & W work caboose; 12 curved, 3 straight, 6149, 1025 transformer.

Comments: This outfit was almost the same as catalogued outfit 11540. As did 11540, this set came in a Type D display-style box, but it included the 6162 as an extra item of rolling stock. The addition of the canister car and a Figure 8 track plan to the outfit probably accounts for the -500 suffix. Perhaps Lionel was approached by a customer who was hesitant to buy, and as a "pot sweetener," agreed to change the contents; a struggling business becomes very flexible when a sale is pending.

The 1966 edition of the 6473 rodeo car surfaces with maroon lettering and the final modification to the shell of this item. Note that the 6473 is heat stamped "HORSE TRANSPORT CAR", but an original box and the catalogue reference *always* describe the item as rodeo car. J. Algozzini Collection.   **125   275**

11570   1966

Contents: 1061 steam locomotive; (1061T) unstamped slope-back tender; (6402) gray General-type flatcar with cable reels; (6042) blue unstamped gondola; (6167) red unstamped SP-type caboose; 8 curved, 2 straight, 1025 transformer.

Comments: This was an extremely low-end set that had a consist of unstamped rolling stock, and that alone makes it collectible. Interestingly, this set has been observed in two types of outfit boxes. The first box was a miniature white conventional two-tier type with orange lettering while the other was a Type D display style; needless to say, none of the contents were component boxed. Note that the outfit number fits into Lionel's numbering sequence for catalogued sets; 11560 was the last O27 outfit number used in 1965 while 11590 was the first new catalogued number used in 1966. W. Stitt Collection.   **75   175**

11620   1968

Contents: 2029 steam locomotive; 234T square tender; (6476) yellow Lehigh Valley hopper; (6402) gray General-type flatcar with cable reels; 6062-50 black gondola without load; 6130 Santa Fe work caboose; 8 curved, 1 straight, 6149, 1025 transformer.

At first glance, this 1968 set may be dismissed as simply another bland steam freight outfit, but it is definitely much more fascinating than it appears. The 2029 was made in Japan, and the tender had "234W" heat stamped on the shell, even though it was not a whistle tender. Of particular interest is this outfit number. It is in the 11600 series and fits perfectly into the catalogued sequence. The 1968 Hagerstown set was numbered "11600" while the introductory 1969 outfit was "11710". A. Tolli Collection.

VG   LN

Comments: The outfit box was a conventional tan two-tier type with unboxed components. The rolling stock was run-of-the-mill for the period and would hardly raise an eyebrow, but this set *is* much more interesting than it first appears. The 2029 engine was made in Japan and is identical to the Hagerstown engine included with catalogued set 11600. The tender had "234W" heat stamped on the shell even though it was *not* a whistle tender, hence the 234T nomenclature. The gondola, with late AAR trucks and no load, is the same as what was catalogued as 6062-50 in 1969! And there's still more: the hopper was unnumbered, yet given a 6476 designation because it had *two* operating couplers, and the common-as-lint gray General-type flatcar also had two operating couplers with late AAR trucks, which indicates that it was 1968-1969 production.

Another notable feature of this set is the set number itself. It is in the 11600 series, which fits into the sequence of numbers for catalogued sets (e.g., the 1968 Hagerstown set number was 11600 and the introductory 1969 outfit was 11710). We suspect that outfits 11610, 11630, 11640, 11650, 11660, 11670, 11680, 11690, and 11700 also exist. B. Myles, F. Davis and A. Tolli Collections.   **225**   **400**

This outfit typifies some of the problems inherent with the study of uncatalogued sets. The Van Camp boxcar was originally issued as part of 1962 outfit 19142, yet here it appears in a set with a lower outfit number, which implies earlier release. The contents of outfit 19000 date to late 1962 or 1963. It "should" have been numbered in either the high 19100s or 19200s. Also, note the presence of factory-stamped "2893" which appears below the outfit number. Was it the stock number for a retail store? Maybe it was a type of dating code from Lionel used for means of further identification. Could it translate to the 28th day of the 9th month in the year '63? M. Toth Collection.

	VG	LN

19000 / 2893   1962

Contents: 1060 steam locomotive; 1060T stream-lined tender; (6502) black flatcar with girder; 6042 blue gondola with cable reels; 638-2361 Van Camp boxcar; (6167) red unstamped SP-type caboose; 8 curved, 2 straight, 1010 transformer.

Comments: This particular set with a 19000 outfit number is definitely out of sequence, since the Van Camp boxcar was originally issued in outfit 19142. To further cloud the issue, we have no explanation for number 2893 at this time. All components came with fixed coupler, arch bar trucks. The black 6502 and the gondola with cable reels were also included with the introductory 1962 catalogued outfit 11201. M. Toth Collection. **100   200**

	VG	LN

19110   1962

Contents: 242 steam locomotive; 1060T stream-lined tender; 3357 cop and hobo car; 6062 gondola with cable reels; 6825 flatcar with trestle; 6057 SP-type caboose; 8 curved, 2 straight, 1008 camtrol, 1010 transformer.

Comments: The outfit box was a generic tan conventional two-tier type with unboxed contents. Except for the tender with arch bar trucks, all components came with AAR trucks and operating couplers. The most interesting item in this otherwise uninteresting set is the cop and hobo car; the parts needed to operate the car were component boxed in a miniature carton numbered "3357-23". K. Rubright Collection. **125   250**

Uncatalogued outfit 19110 from 1962 was headed by the ever-so-common 242 Scout-series steam engine. The set is for the most part uninspiring, but it did contain a slightly better freight roster than most other promotional sets from the era. Note the miniature tan box in the upper left quadrant of the photo; it contained the miscellaneous pieces for the 3357 cop and hobo car, and was numbered "3357-23". Later issues of this box were numbered "3357-27". K. Rubright Collection.

VG   LN

19142   **1962**

Contents: 242 steam locomotive; 1060T streamlined tender; (3309) turbo missile launcher; (6406) maroon General-type flatcar with gray-bumpered auto; 638-2361 Van Camp boxcar; (6167) red unstamped SP-type caboose; 8 curved, 2 straight, 1010 transformer.

Comments: This was a special set orchestrated as an advertising vehicle by Stokely-Van Camp. The outfit box was a conventional tan two-tier type with unboxed components separated by cardboard dividers. The set was offered for $11.95 on the label from a can of pork and beans. The 242 engine stirs minimal interest, but this is one of the more desirable of the promotional sets due in part to its unique background and the inclusion of the Van Camp boxcar. Mixed coupler and truck types were the norm. Verified examples of this set all contain a yellow auto, but other colors could well have been used. This set also included the three-cut billboard sheet with a Van Camp billboard, probably required as per the business agreement. Note that the Van Camp boxcar was also a component of several other sets; evidently supply exceeded demand. Also note that it was listed in the *Lionel Service Manual* as "6050-150". Please refer to outfits 19142-100 and 19142-502. V. Bibelot and P. Ambrose Collections.   **225**   **500**

19142-100   **1962**

Comments: This outfit was identical to the above listed Van Camp set 19142, but for some unknown reason the outfit box had a "-100" suffix as part of the set number. R. Larson and J. Algozzini Collections.   **225**   **500**

19142-502   **1963**

Contents: 242 steam locomotive; (1061T) unstamped slope-back tender; (6406) maroon General-type flatcar with gray-bumpered auto; 6014 white Frisco boxcar; 3830 flatcar with operating submarine; (6120) yellow unstamped work caboose; uncut sheet of 12 Lionel collec-

Outfit 19142-100 is known as the Van Camp set. It was a special 1962 promotional outfit assembled as an advertising vehicle for Stokely-Van Camp. The contents are by no means scarce, but as a total package, this is a very collectible set that included the first issue of the 638-2361 Van Camp boxcar. The set was offered for $11.95 on the label from a can of pork and beans. Observe that the outfit pictured above came in a set carton with a -100 suffix. We cannot explain why a suffix was used when an identical set was available in a box numbered only "19142". A variation of this outfit also exists in an outfit box marked with a -502 suffix. J. Algozzini Collection.

tor cards; cardstock punch-out sheet with railroad-related items; 12 curved, 4 straight, 1008 camtrol, 90° crossing, 1010 transformer.

Comments: This is a difficult set to analyze because the outfit box was the same as was used for the Van Camp set, with a -502 suffix added; refer to sets 19142 and 19142-100. This was probably an effort by Lionel to deplete partially assembled sets with on-hand, overstocked inventory. The component-boxed 3830 was a premium car with an $8.95 separate-sale price while the other items bordered on low end. Lionel may have even pulled the Van Camp boxcar from already assembled sets and substituted a Frisco boxcar to distinguish this variation from 19142. Evidence shows that Lionel still had unsold inventory on

                                                        VG   LN

the Van Camp boxcar—it has been reported in other uncatalogued sets. Note that this outfit dates to 1963 while 19142 and 19142-100 were from 1962. S. Bradley Collection.   **275   600**

***

19147   **1962**

Contents: 1060 steam locomotive; 1060T streamlined tender; 6480 exploding boxcar; (3309) turbo missile launcher; 6042 blue gondola without load; (6167) red unstamped SP-type caboose; 8 curved, 2 straight, 1026 transformer.

Comments: Even though low end, this uncatalogued outfit was at least as good as the first outfit

The contents pictured above belong with 1963 outfit 19142-502. For comparison, we have also shown only the set box for outfit 19142, which was the 1962 issue of the Van Camp set. Although the contents for set 19142-502 are almost completely different from the items shown with set 19142-100 in the color photo of that set, Lionel retained the same basic outfit number. Why? Maybe because they were headed by the same 242 engine. Most unfortunately, due to an oversight on our part, we failed to photograph the sheet of Lionel collector cards and the cardstock punch-out sheet of railroad-related items that were included with outfit 19142-502; the identical punch-out sheet, however, is shown in the color photo for set 19328. S. Bradley Collection.

	VG	LN

featured in the 1962 Lionel consumer catalogue. All components came with fixed coupler, arch bar trucks and were packaged unboxed in a generic tan outfit carton. The 6480 exploding boxcar was an uncatalogued set component and is far more collectible than the 6470, which was the catalogued version. D. Cirillo Collection. **100 225**

19185   1962

Contents: 242 steam locomotive. Please refer to Spiegel outfit 5278.

19203X   1963

Contents: 243 steam locomotive; 1130T streamlined tender; 6343 barrel ramp car; 6062 gondola with cable reels; 3362 helium tank unloading car; 6057-50 orange SP-type caboose; 8 curved, 2 straight, 1008 camtrol, 1025 transformer.

Comments: The outfit box was a tan conventional two-tier type. All of the components came with early AAR trucks, and were packaged in a boxed/unboxed combination along with cardboard dividers. No specific item

Outfit 19216 is dated to 1963, yet it is headed by the 1065 Union Pacific Alco A unit that debuted in 1961 advance catalogue set 1125. This outfit also contained a Van Camp boxcar; however, the best item in the set is the orange two-dome Lionel Lines tank car that is numbered "6045". It is exceptionally scarce and often overlooked by collectors because it is nearly identical to the catalogued version numbered "6465". Though low end, this is an extremely colorful outfit, and color, then and now, facilitates the sale of trains. P. Michael Collection.

	VG	LN

generates collector interest, but the orange 6057 is one of the better late SP-type cabooses. Reported to B. Greenberg, collector unknown.

100   225

19212 — 1963

Contents: 242 steam locomotive; 1060T streamlined tender; 6014 white Frisco boxcar; 3410 flatcar with operating helicopter; (6406) gray General-type flatcar with gray-bumpered auto; 6059 red M St. L SP-type caboose; 12 curved, 4 straight, 90° crossing, 1010 transformer.

Comments: This set came in a Type A display-style outfit box with 1963 graphics. The tender and flatcar came with arch bar trucks while the other items came with AAR trucks and had one fixed and one operating coupler. As reported, the outfit contained a scarce brown auto and a solid yellow helicopter. Unfortunately for collectors and historians, Lionel did not use color consistently on accent

pieces such as helicopters, autos or cable reels, and this set may surface with variations. C. Swanson Collection.

225   450

19216 — 1963

Contents: 1065 Union Pacific Alco A unit; 638-2361 Van Camp boxcar; 6062 gondola with cable reels; 6045 orange Lionel Lines tank car; (6167) red unstamped SP-type caboose; 12 curved, 4 straight, 90° crossing, 1025 transformer.

Comments: Where do all the Van Camp boxcars come from, you ask? They come from numerous uncatalogued sets in addition to the original issue that came in outfit 19142. Set 19216 was the result of further housecleaning at the Lionel factory. The 1065 Union Pacific was originally issued with 1961 advance catalogue set 1125, and by 1963, was without doubt "stagnant" shelf inventory. (The same can be said for the 6062 gondola that debuted in 1959.) The 1065 is collectible, but the best item

Would you believe another outfit with a Van Camp boxcar? Lionel must have thought that every family in America was going to order a Van Camp set! Nonetheless, this 1963 outfit prompts curiosity. Note the unusual number that appears immediately below the outfit number. Although suffixes are quite common with uncatalogued sets, we have never seen the use of 108-105 anywhere before. P. Michael Collection.

VG   LN

in the set is the scarce Lionel Lines tank car with arch bar trucks that was numbered "6045" instead of "6465".

The outfit box was a conventional tan two-tier type that came with unboxed components separated by cardboard dividers. P. Michael Collection.   **150   300**

19219 / 108-105   1963

Contents: 211P/211T Texas Special Alco AA units; 638-2361 Van Camp boxcar; 6042 blue gondola with cable reels; 6076 red Lehigh Valley hopper; (6502) blue unstamped flatcar with girder; (6167) brown unstamped SP-type caboose; 110 trestle set; 17 curved, 10 straight, 1008 camtrol, 1025 transformer.

Comments: The outfit box was a conventional tan two-tier type that came with unboxed components, except that it was oversized to accommodate the boxed trestle piers (see outfit 19225 for an explanation of the "odd"

VG   LN

quantity of track). Of particular interest is the 108-105 number that appears to have been stamped by Lionel as part of the set number. Except for the gondola which had AAR trucks, all components came with fixed coupler, arch bar trucks. An unstamped SP-type caboose in brown is a scarce example. This was yet another set to include the Van Camp boxcar, listed in the *Lionel Service Manual* as "6050-150", that was originally commissioned for outfit 19142. Were sales on outfit 19142 that much below projection? D. Miller and P. Michael Collections.   **225   450**

19220   1963

Contents: 1061 steam locomotive; (1061T) unstamped slope-back tender; (6502) blue unstamped flatcar with girder; 638-2361 Van Camp boxcar; (6167) red unstamped SP-type caboose; 8 curved, 2 straight, 1026 transformer.

This outfit was undoubtedly one of the best uncatalogued offerings in 1963. The 211 Texas Special Alco units provided motive power for the mostly red consist of military-related rolling stock. Look carefully at the black flatcar; notice the rare white-over-red Beechcraft Bonanza airplane. It is utterly amazing that Lionel packaged this outfit without a single component box to protect the fragile military items; all items were separated and held in place by cardboard dividers. J. Amanda Collection.

VG   LN

Comments: The outfit box was a miniature version of the tan conventional two-tier type. The components were unboxed and had varying combinations of trucks and couplers. This was a very low-end set that was similar to advance catalogued outfit 11415. The inclusion of the 638-2361 was probably no more than an effort by Lionel to deplete excess inventory remaining from the special Van Camp promotion of 1962. Refer to outfit 19142. Reported by I. D. Smith.   **75   150**

19225   1963

Contents: 211P/211T Texas Special Alco AA units; 6448 exploding boxcar; (6500) flatcar with airplane; (6501) flatcar with jet motorboat; 6650 flatcar with IRBM launcher; (6167) red unstamped SP-type caboose; 110 trestle set; 17 curved, 10 straight, 1008 camtrol, 1025 transformer.

Comments: The outfit box was an oversized tan conventional two-tier type. The odd track assortment and the trestle set provided a unique layout. Seventeen curved sections are not quite mathematically correct, but this unique "over and under" track diagram (No. 1802I) specifies seventeen curved track. For example, one portion of the diagram calls for the use of four curved sections which equate to a 180° turn (or one-half circle), yet the turn diagramed is only about 160°! Fortunately, O27 Gauge track is pliable enough to allow for minor miscalculations.

The Texas Special was reissued in 1962 as 211 and headed a total of three catalogued sets. The rolling stock was quite impressive (and expensive) for an uncatalogued set. This set contained the very desirable white-over-red airplane on an unnumbered black flatcar that was also a component of 1962 catalogued set 13018, and the scarce jet motorboat car. All components were unboxed and came with early AAR trucks and operating couplers at both ends, except for the low-end 6167 caboose, which had one fixed coupler. J. Amanda Collection.   **600   1300**

An uneducated buyer may dismiss this set as not worth owning, but the astute collector would immediately spot a "jewel." The green "premium" automobile with gray bumpers is a prize; it alone is worth approximately $300 in today's market. Outfit 19228 is dated to 1963; note that many 1963 sets included both a consumer and accessory catalogue along with a three-cut billboard sheet as part of outfit packaging. Look closely at the unstamped slope-back tender. In 1963 Lionel further reduced assembly costs by eliminating the slot and screw frame in favor of a galvanized bend-down tab frame. This version of the tender is given 1061T nomenclature; if fitted with a truck that included an electrically grounded copper spring, it would be referred to as "1062T". J. Algozzini Collection.

VG   LN

19228   1963

Contents: 1062 steam locomotive; (1061T) unstamped slope-back tender; 3410 flatcar with operating helicopter; (6406) gray General-type flatcar with gray-bumpered auto; 6042 gondola with cable reels; (6167) red unstamped SP-type caboose; 8 curved, 2 straight, 1010 transformer.

Comments: The manually operated 3410 helicopter car with a yellow "chopper" (the same as was included with the 419 heliport) is a very collectible item, but the "jewel" from this set is the green auto (refer to comments on outfit 19262). The General-type flatcar had its humble beginning in 1959 with the introduction of the 1877 flatcar with horses. The next issue was the 1887, followed by a black example, stamped "6404", that debuted with a gray-bumpered auto (colors varied) as a component of 1960

advance catalogue set 1109. Lionel's follow-up to the 6404 was the maroon 6405 flatcar with van and an unstamped maroon example that was a frequent component of un-catalogued sets in 1961 and 1962; it was referred to in the *Lionel Service Manual* as a 6406 with yellow auto. As soon as the maroon was depleted, it was replaced throughout the entire product line with gray. Gray flatcars were used continuously through the remainder of the postwar era and appear with varying types of trucks and couplers. Note that the 3410 from this set was a lighter blue molded plastic than that which was used for the earlier run, and this example had one fixed and one operating coupler.

The set box was a tan conventional two-tier type. Be advised that Lionel usually included both a consumer and an accessory catalogue as part of 1963 outfit packaging. J. Algozzini Collection.   **325**   **700**

This 1963 outfit was "Spartan." One of the methods employed by Lionel to reduce production costs was to eliminate heat stamping. Such unstamped rolling stock has become quite collectible in recent times. None of the items in set 19260 are difficult to obtain, but an unstamped brown SP-type caboose is somewhat scarce and often overlooked by collectors. A Tolli Collection.

	VG	LN

19244   1963

Contents: 1061 steam locomotive; (1061T) unstamped slope-back tender; 6042 blue gondola with canisters; (6402) gray General-type flatcar with cable reels; (6167) red unstamped SP-type caboose; 8 curved, 4 straight, 1026 transformer.

Comments: This outfit came with unboxed contents in a miniature tan conventional two-tier set box. The roster of contents could hardly turn one's head. The rolling stock was the least expensive Lionel had to offer and came with varying combinations of arch bar and AAR trucks. This set was very similar to 1962 advance catalogue outfit 11001. C. Swanson Collection.

75   125

	VG	LN

19247   1963

Contents: 1061 steam locomotive; (1061T) unstamped slope-back tender; 6042 blue gondola with canisters; (6409) red flatcar with two brown autos; (6167) brown unstamped SP-type caboose; 8 curved, 2 straight, 1026 transformer.

Comments: The outfit box was a plain tan conventional two-tier type with unboxed contents. This set was extremely "low end," yet it has some very collectible items, namely the brown autos and a brown unstamped SP-type caboose. The (6409) was a Lionel-lettered full-sized flatcar without a superstructure. To date, this is the only known instance in which a flatcar, along with two gray-bumpered autos, was offered in a promotional set. F. Wasserman Collection.

400   850

Even at first glance, one's eyes are immediately drawn to the scarce brown automobile sitting atop the General-type flatcar. With further study of 1963 outfit 19262, one will notice a roster of mostly unstamped components, the least expensive Lionel could produce, yet a "better" operating car, the 3357 that had a separate-sale price of $7.95, was included! The blue 3357 is stamped "Hydraulic Platform Maintenance Car"; however, the miniature tan box numbered "3357-27" that contained the necessary trestle components refers to the 3357 as cop and hobo car. Such contradictions could exist only in the realm of Lionel. K. Rubright Collection.

	VG	LN

19260   1963

Contents: 1061 steam locomotive; (1061T) un-stamped slope-back tender; (6042) blue unstamped gon-dola; (6076) gray unstamped hopper; (6409) flatcar with pipes; (6167) brown unstamped SP-type caboose; 8 curved, 2 straight, 1026 transformer.

Comments: The contents of this outfit were about as humble as one could get from Lionel, yet it was a grade above catalogued "starter" outfit 11311 because it in-cluded an extra car. Though Spartan even by 1963 stand-ards, unstamped rolling stock has become quite collectible in recent times. The brown unstamped SP-type caboose is the best item in the set.

There seems to have been a proliferation of un-catalogued sets in 1963. The outfit box was the same as most others—a tan conventional two-tier type. A. Tolli Collection.   **125**   **250**

	VG	LN

19260-500   1963

Contents: 1061 steam locomotive; (1062T) un-stamped slope-back tender; (6042) blue unstamped gon-dola; (6076) gray unstamped hopper; (6167) red unstamped SP-type caboose; 12 curved, 4 straight, 90° crossing, 1026 transformer.

Comments: This outfit was nearly the same as the above mentioned set and came in an identical outfit carton that had a -500 suffix added. Apparently Lionel depleted their stock on the 6409 flatcar with pipes and decided to further amend the outfit by including a Figure 8 track plan. R. Okun Collection.   **100**   **200**

19262   1963

Contents: 237 steam locomotive; (1062T) un-stamped slope-back tender; 3357 cop and hobo car; (6076)

Outfit 19263 is called "The Libby Set"; it is one of the best of the promotional sets. At the time of issue, all components, except the 1062 engine, were exclusive to this outfit. Like the Van Camp set from 1962, this outfit also failed to meet sales expectations. Subsequently, each item appeared in other uncatalogued sets, and the 6167 Union Pacific caboose was ultimately depleted as a catalogued set component in 1969! Pay particular attention to the streamlined tender; it is a very scarce example lettered "SOUTHERN PACIFIC", not the usual "Lionel Lines". W. Pike Collection.

VG   LN

gray unstamped hopper; (6406) gray General-type flatcar with gray-bumpered auto; (6167) brown unstamped SP-type caboose; 12 curved, 4 straight, 90° crossing, 1010 transformer.

Comments: The outfit box was a plain tan conventional two-tier type with unboxed contents. The components came with varying truck and coupler combinations; note that this unpretentious set did not even include a camtrol. However, in today's market, what have become two very collectible items are part of this set—a gray-bumpered auto and an unstamped brown SP-type caboose.

Colors of accent pieces such as automobiles, cable reels and canisters varied depending upon in-stock position. Green, brown and yellow gray-bumpered autos are all in collector demand; this set usually contained a brown

example. Automobile colors are rated as follows: green (rare), brown (very scarce), yellow (fairly common), and red (most common). Many of the sets that contained a gray-bumpered auto have had their contents altered. Entire sets have often been purchased by knowledgeable collectors for a price considerably less than the value of a single automobile. Rare and scarce autos have been replaced by common ones, and the sets have then been resold for purchase price, with the net gain of a "free" green or brown auto. J. Amanda and S. Bradley Collections. **275   600**

19263   **1963**

Contents: 1062 steam locomotive; 1060T streamlined tender lettered "SOUTHERN PACIFIC"; 6076 ATSF hopper; 6050 Libby's Tomato Juice boxcar; 6475 Libby's vat car; 6167 Union Pacific SP-type caboose; 8 curved, 2 straight, 1010 transformer.

Comments: This is one of the best of the promotional sets; it has come to be known simply as "The Libby Set." The outfit box was a conventional tan two-tier type with unboxed components. The 1062 is very common and of minimal value, but the other components, especially the Southern Pacific tender, are all very desirable collector items. The tender is given 1060T nomenclature because it is on an arch bar truck frame with a fixed coupler. The 6475 is known to have come in either the light aqua (scarce) or the more common shade of medium blue plastic. Truck types vary and most components came with fixed couplers.

Evidently this set also failed to meet sales expectations because each item is a known component of several other promotional sets. The 6167 Union Pacific caboose first appeared in 1963, but was ultimately depleted as a catalogued set component in 1969; unmounted 6167 shells

Pictured here is one end (opposite the outfit number) of set carton 19281. Note the Shell shipping label and metered postage on the carton. Was this set somehow associated with Shell Oil Company? Another set, purchased at Madison Hardware by A. Vincent in the early 1980s, does not show the Shell logo on the outfit box. P. Michael Collection.

Lionel must have been running a "fire sale" on trestle sets in 1963. Outfit 19281 is one of several sets from the product year to utilize the same generic tan oversized outfit box and incorporate an "over and under" track plan with a graduated trestle set. This set was headed by the 231 Rock Island Alco A unit, another sales disappointment. The 231 headed one catalogued gift pack in 1961, but was listed for separate sale in 1962 and 1963, and was frequently motive power for uncatalogued sets. The example illustrated above has a Shell shipping label affixed to the opposite end of the set carton. P. Michael Collection.

By its roster, 1964 outfit 19328 would be deemed inconsequential; however, focus on the gray cable reels and the cardstock punch-out sheet of railroad-related items. The set carton proudly states, "MANUFACTURED and GUARANTEED BY THE LIONEL CORPORATION, NEW YORK, N.Y.", but the cardstock sheet was marked "Printed in Japan" and does not carry the Lionel logo. It is a rare paper collectible but is not unique to this set. Several other outfits from 1963 and 1964 included the same sheet. R. Corruthers Collection.

	VG	LN

are still available in the marketplace. W. Pike and P. Ambrose Collections.   **350**   **700**

19281   1963

Contents: 231 Rock Island Alco A unit; (3309) or (3349) turbo missile launcher; (6502) blue unstamped flatcar with girder; (6402) gray General-type flatcar with cable reels; (6076) gray unstamped hopper; 6473 rodeo car; 6017 SP-type caboose; 110 trestle set; 12 curved, 14 straight, 1008 camtrol, 1025 transformer,

Comments: The outfit box was a slightly oversized tan conventional two-tier type. Curiously, one end of the

set carton (opposite the outfit number) had a Shell shipping label attached. Could this set have been associated with the Shell Oil Company? The trestle set was component boxed while the other unboxed items were separated by cardboard dividers. By the roster of contents, it appears that this was another set assembled solely to move overstocked inventory. The 231 was introduced in 1961 and headed one catalogued set, yet it continued to be listed for separate sale through 1963. It provided motive power for several other uncatalogued sets. This set has also been reported to contain an 1877 flatcar with horses in lieu of the 6402. Available evidence suggests that the 1877 was produced in 1959 and possibly 1960, yet here it sometimes appears in a 1963 set. The inclusion of the 1877 is plausible because it was similar

This nondescript 1964 set was Lionel uncatalogued outfit 19350. It was probably available to any retailer willing to place an order with Lionel, but it was also obtainable through S & H, the Chicago-based Green Stamp house. In addition to the number 19350, "6P4811" was rubber stamped on the side of the set box lid. Note that the manual release 3410 helicopter launching car from this outfit came with a scarce yellow "chopper" that was originally issued with the 419 heliport accessory. J. Algozzini Collection.

VG   LN

in appearance and cost, and was from the same period. Along with the other "General" items, it was a sales laggard. Keep in mind that one of the functions of uncatalogued sets was to deplete overstocked existing inventory. A. Vincent and P. Michael Collections. **200**   **425**

19325   **1964**

Contents: 1061 steam locomotive. Kindly refer to Sears set 9813 for further information.

This 1964 outfit was also available through Sperry and Hutchinson (S & H). It utilized the Lionel outfit number 19350 but included a -500 suffix as well. Outfit 19350-500 also employed the same 6P4811 number as did set 19350, but is a much more desirable set because it included the rare 240 Scout-series steam engine along with the dark yellow variation of the 3619 helicopter reconnaissance car. The 6402 General-type flatcar carried a load of two cable reels; for purposes of illustration, it is shown in the picture with the red helicopter that belongs with the 3619. R. Mack Collection.

19328   1964

Contents: 1061 steam locomotive; 1060T streamlined tender; 6465 orange Lionel Lines tank car; 6014 white Frisco boxcar; 6142 gondola with cable reels; 6167 SP-type caboose; uncut sheet of 12 Lionel collector cards; cardstock punch-out sheet with railroad-related items; 12 curved, 4 straight, 1008 camtrol, 90° crossing, 1026 transformer.

Comments: This outfit came with unboxed components in a conventional two-tier white set box with orange lettering that was introduced late in the 1964 product year. Ironically, the entire roster of catalogued O27 sets came in Type D display-style boxes during 1964, yet this low-end uncatalogued set came in a new-issue white box that was developed for the O Gauge line.

The engine and rolling stock barely deserve comment, but the miscellaneous paper accessories are indeed

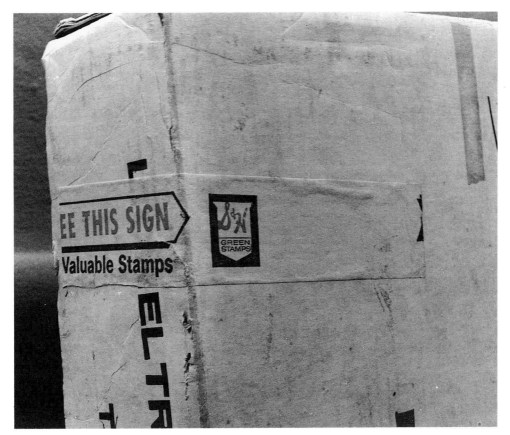

This detailed photograph shows one corner of outfit box 19350-500/6P4811 and highlights the S & H Green Stamp sealing tape. R. Mack Collection.

	VG	LN

noteworthy. The cardstock sheet was marked "printed in Japan" but did not carry the Lionel logo. For reasons we have not discovered, several other outfits from the 1963-1964 era have been observed with the same miscellany, but they were incomplete sets and are not listed in this edition. R. Corruthers and B. Myles Collections.

225   500

19333   1964

Contents: 1062 steam locomotive. See listing for J. C. Penney outfit 0664.

19334   1964

Contents: 221 U.S.M.C. Alco A unit. Refer to J. C. Penney set 0680.

19341   1964

Contents: 221 Rio Grande Alco A unit; 3362/64 operating log car; 6142 blue gondola with canisters; 6076 black Lehigh Valley hopper; 6167 SP-type caboose; 8 curved, 3 straight, 6149, 1010 transformer.

Comments: This set came in a Type D display-style outfit box with 1964 orange and white graphics. It was very similar to catalogued outfit 11440, with only the 3362/64 replacing the (3309) turbo missile launcher. Unassuming sets such as this one, with easily obtained contents, pique minimal interest among advanced collectors unless they are absolutely pristine. K. Rubright Collection.

150   300

19350 / 6P4811   1964

Contents: 242 steam locomotive; 1060T streamlined tender; 6476 red Lehigh Valley hopper; 3410 flatcar with operating helicopter; (6408) flatcar with pipes; 6059 red M St. L SP-type caboose; 8 curved, 5 straight, 6149, 1010 transformer.

Comments: This set came in a Type D display-style outfit box with orange 1964 graphics. The inclusion of the 6P4811 implies that this set was available through Sperry and Hutchinson even though S & H does not appear with the number.

By 1964 Lionel was deeply engaged in depleting existing inventory; the 3410 with yellow helicopter is testimony to that activity. The rolling stock came with varying truck combinations; and all items except the tender came with one operating coupler. This is a

VG   LN

desirable set for the advanced collector. The contents are widely available but the true prize is the outfit box itself. Refer to set 19350-500 for more information. J. Algozzini Collection.   **150   325**

19350-500 / 6P-4811 or 6P4811   1964

Contents: 240 steam locomotive; 242T streamlined tender; 6176 gray Lehigh Valley hopper; (6402) gray General-type flatcar with cable reels; 3619 reconnaissance copter car; 6059 red M St. L SP-type caboose; 12 curved, 3 straight, 6149, 90° crossing, 1010 transformer.

Comments: This set also came with unboxed contents in a Type D display-style box with 1964 graphics, and was also stamped "6P-4811", implying that it was available through Sperry and Hutchinson (refer to outfit 19350). The Lionel number was stamped on the left side of the box end while the S & H number appeared on the

right. The photograph of the set from the Mack collection shows the S & H number as "6P4811" without the dash. This set was probably assembled to deplete excess inventory on the 240 engine that had originally been made for Sears to head outfit 9820. Truck and coupler types varied. New 1964 items had late AAR trucks with open journal boxes (axle ends visible), while the carryover 3619 and 6059 still had early AAR trucks (closed journal boxes). Most cars in this outfit had couplers with the copper-molded leaf spring whose use was most prevalent in 1963-1964. Also note that it contained an expensive ($10.95) premium car, the 3619, which was quite unusual for an uncatalogued set. The inclusion of the 3619, most often the scarce dark yellow variation, is plausible because by 1964 it was an overstocked, "dead" item, and was listed for separate sale only. This outfit is prized by collectors because of the scarcity of the outfit box itself, as well as the 240 engine, one of the rarest in the Scout series. D. Miller and R. Mack Collections.

The rolling stock consist of this 1964 outfit was ill conceived—the olive drab items just do not relate to the other components. Evidently Lionel was drowning in inventory, and assembled this outfit solely to move shelf stock. Even the 6470 exploding boxcar was antiquated; although it was replaced by the similar two-tone 6448 in 1961, it was still catalogued through 1962. The size of the outfit box and the -500 suffix leads us to believe that this set may have included a 110 graduated trestle set or other miscellaneous items similar to what was included with outfit 19567-500. C. Hurschik Collection.

	VG	LN

We also have a report from D. Cirillo in which packaging and contents are the same as listed above, except that the Cirillo outfit was headed by an extremely common 246 engine. Almost anything is plausible in reference to uncatalogued sets. Perhaps Lionel depleted existing inventory on the 246 engine, then substituted the 240 engine to complete the order for S & H. Back in 1964, these engines were one in the same to Lionel; both were inexpensive steam engines with plastic boilers, ideal candidates for an uncatalogued set.

	VG	LN
With 240 engine	350	800
With 246 engine	200	450

19351-500   1964

Contents: 239 steam locomotive; 242T streamlined tender; 6162 gondola with canisters; 6470 exploding boxcar; (6402) gray General-type flatcar with cable reels; (6176-100) olive drab unstamped hopper; (6119-125) olive drab "RESCUE UNIT" medical caboose; track and transformer unknown.

Comments: This intriguing set came with unboxed contents in an oversized conventional two-tier tan outfit box. The underside of the box is dated "1963" above the United Container seal, but this outfit dates to 1964. The size of the outfit box and a -500 suffix suggests the inclusion of other miscellaneous items (unknown at this time) such as those that came with set 19567-500.

The contents were a hodgepodge that included olive drab military items from the era, low-end general merchandise, and even a 6470 that was last catalogued in 1962. Trucks and coupler types were extremely varied while the die-cast 239 engine was the heat-stamped variation. C. Hurschik Collection.   250   525

19371   1964

Contents: 237 steam locomotive. Please refer to Spiegel set 5284.

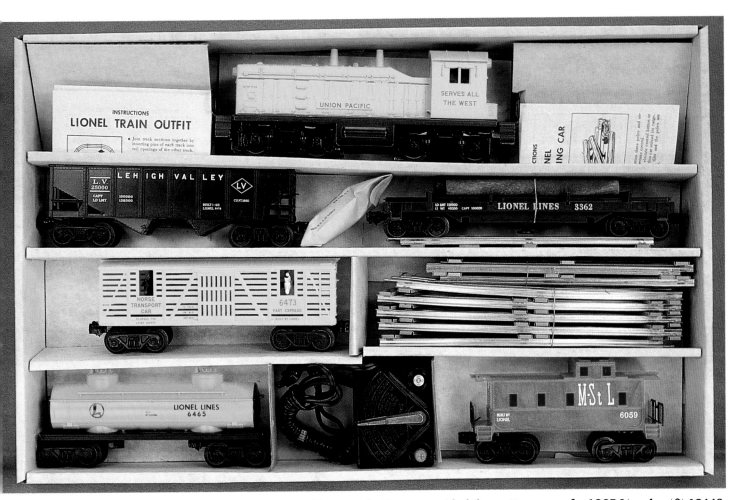

The 635 Union Pacific diesel switcher was uncatalogued by Lionel. Here it provided the motive power for 1965 Lionel outfit 19440. The rolling stock was mediocre at best, but it was indeed colorful. During a period in which Lionel was cutting production costs to the bone, they sustained the expense of painting the 635 cab. Lionel did not do it out of the kindness of its heart; they were "forced" to paint the 635 because it came on a gray body mold, which, unless painted, was of no use to Lionel. A. Vincent Collection.

VG   LN

19394   1964

Contents: 227 Canadian National Alco A unit; (6502) blue unstamped flatcar with girder; (6042) blue unstamped gondola with canisters; 638-2361 Van Camp boxcar; (6167) red unstamped SP-type caboose; 16 curved, 4 straight, 45° crossing, 1026 transformer.

Comments: It is truly amazing what can be found in an uncatalogued set. This outfit was headed by the 227 Alco unit that first appeared four years earlier in set 1115, and contained yet another Van Camp boxcar; however, this was no ordinary Van Camp boxcar. The 638-2361 was a light red variation on a Type 3 body mold. Apparently Lionel had an agreement with Stokely-Van Camp to continue marketing a boxcar that promoted their name and product. Could this set have been a second Van Camp promotion aimed at the Canadian market? It seems likely, especially with the Canadian National Alco and when the generic tan two-tier outfit carton was rubber stamped

"Include 910 billboard with this set". We cannot identify what the 910 number indicated, but a three-cut sheet that included the Van Camp billboard was packaged in the outfit carton. L. Harold Collection.   275   550

19427   1965

Contents: 1061 steam locomotive; (1061T) unstamped slope-back tender; 6042 black gondola with canisters; (6502) blue unstamped flatcar with black girder; (6167) yellow unstamped SP-type caboose; 8 curved, 1010 transformer.

Comments: Lionel did not make many outfits that were less expensive than this one. The outfit box was a miniature tan two-tier type with unboxed contents. Yellow unstamped SP-type cabooses are considerably more difficult to find than red examples, and as a pleasant surprise, this outfit contained a collectible black girder as

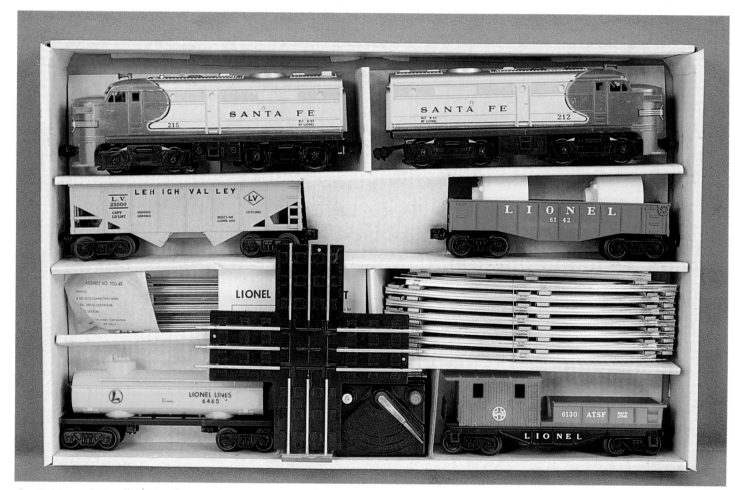

Outfit 19444 from 1965 was headed by the 215P/212T Santa Fe Alco units; Lionel intended to make this mixed pairing. The 215 variation of the war bonnet Santa Fe Alco was strictly an uncatalogued engine; it was the poor cousin, one without a horn, to the catalogued 212. Lionel ceased to equip their Alcos with Magnetraction in 1962; most post-1962 Alco-powered units were fitted instead with a weight riveted to the rear of the cab for additional traction. Lionel did not deem it necessary nor did they wish to incur the expense of adding the weight to dummy or trailer units. Since all 215 cabs were manufactured with the weight, they were usually mated with a non-weighted 212T unit. This identical roster in a different type of set box was also catalogued by Spiegel in 1965 as outfit 5263. V. Bibelot Collection.

Outfit 19444-502, like outfit 19444, was powered by a 215 Santa Fe Alco, but this variation of the set paired the motorized unit with a 218C B unit. To further differentiate the outfit, there were substitutions of rolling stock and caboose, and set 19444-502 was packaged in a two-tier tan generic outfit carton. The helium tank unloading car included with this set was completely unstamped. This is a legitimate variation, not a factory error. T. Randazzo Collection.

	VG	LN

well. The girder had raised Lionel letters, but they were *not* outlined in white. Apparently the factory cleaned out the 214 girder bridge parts bin as this girder shows no evidence of ever being riveted to a bridge plate. Reported by E. Prendeville. **75 175**

19428 1965

Contents: 1061 steam locomotive; 1061T slope-back tender; (6042) blue unstamped gondola; (6167) red unstamped SP-type caboose; 12 curved, 4 straight, 90° crossing, 1026 transformer.

Comments: This uncatalogued outfit was nearly identical to 1964 Lionel catalogued set 11420, and yes, Lionel did catalogue a set with only one rolling stock item!

	VG	LN

However, this outfit is a shade better than the catalogue offering because it included a Figure 8 track plan. The set carton was a generic tan type that featured the new name change. D. Cirillo Collection. **75 150**

19436 1965

Contents: 1062 steam locomotive; 1062T slope-back tender; 6142 green gondola with canisters; 3362/64 operating log car; 6059 red M St. L SP-type caboose; 12 curved, 3 straight, 6149, 90° crossing, 1010 transformer.

Comments: This "starter" set came in a 1965 Type D display-style outfit box. Because of the inclusion of the operating 3362/64, Lionel included a 6149 remote-controlled track section. In an attempt to glamorize inconsequential contents, Lionel often included a Figure

VG LN

8 track plan. It was no doubt more cost efficient to give both an additional four sections of track at a 1965 retail price of $0.25 per section and a 90° crossing retail priced at $2 than it was to include another piece of rolling stock. K. Rubright Collection. **75 150**

19437 1965

Contents: 237 steam locomotive. See listing for J. C. Penney set 3726.

19438 1965

Contents: 241 steam locomotive. Refer to J. C. Penney outfit 3734.

VG LN

19438-502 1965

Contents: 241 steam locomotive; 234W square whistle tender; 6465 orange Lionel Lines tank car; 6014 white Frisco boxcar; 6176 gray Lehigh Valley hopper; 6059 red M St. L SP-type caboose; track unknown, 147 whistle controller, 1073 transformer.

Contents: The outfit box was a plain tan conventional two-tier type with unboxed contents. The rolling stock is run-of-the-mill, but the 241 is a scarce engine and, in this instance, it was paired with a whistle tender. The 241 was die-cast and an uncatalogued set component only; the boiler casting was shared with the uncatalogued 251 and the catalogued 239 of the same era. Because of the engine, this is one of the more collectible of the low-end steam sets. Reported to B. Greenberg, collector unknown.
175 350

Set 19450 was a typical uncatalogued/promotional set of the mid-1960s. Common-as-dust rolling stock was paired with inexpensive motive power (a 1062 plastic boiler Scout-series engine in this instance) and a Figure 8 track plan. The 6059 M St. L caboose was a component of several catalogued outfits, but it was a staple among uncatalogued sets. Note that this 1965 outfit box still carried the slogan "MANUFACTURED and GUARANTEED BY THE LIONEL CORPORATION, NEW YORK, N.Y." Hillside, New Jersey, would soon replace New York as the base of operations. A. Tolli Collection.

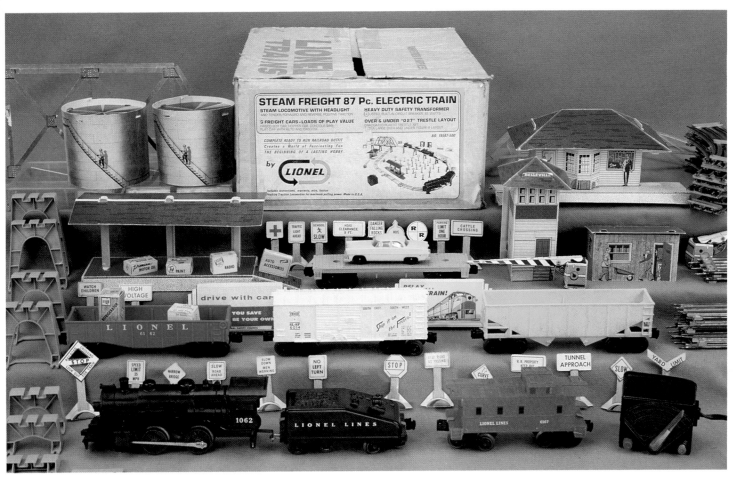

How do we describe this set? Awesome! It almost defies belief that seven inconsequential, regular production Lionel items and 80 miscellaneous pieces, of which most are cardboard punch-outs, make this one of the premier uncatalogued sets, but it's true. We can count on one hand the number of times this outfit has appeared for sale in the marketplace. It does not have anywhere near the distinction of prestige outfits, such as the Halloween General, but it is every bit as rare. An advanced collector would take a third mortgage on his house to obtain an example in pristine condition. J. Algozzini Collection.

	VG	LN

19439   1965

Contents: 1062 steam locomotive; 1062T slope-back tender; 6142 green gondola with canisters; (6402) gray General-type flatcar with cable reels; 6059 red M St. L SP-type caboose; 12 curved, 4 straight, 90° crossing, 1010 transformer.

Comments: Very few collectors would walk across the street to claim this outfit, but an advanced collector would run. This 1965 outfit came in a Type D display-style outfit box that included a G. C. Murphy price sticker that was marked "$11.99". Except for the absence of a 6149 uncoupling section, this outfit is identical to 1965 Spiegel set 5261 that sold through their catalogue at $14.97. Murphy undersold Spiegel by 20 percent! W. Stitt Collection.   **75   175**

19440   1965

Contents: 635 Union Pacific diesel switcher; 6076 black Lehigh Valley hopper; 6473 rodeo car; 6465 orange

This unusual outfit, titled "Pretzel Twin Diesel Freight Train", was 1966 uncatalogued set 19569, which came in a two-tier white conventional set carton with a paste-on label identifying the contents. Most unfortunately, it was not common practice for Lionel to identify the contents of sealed outfit cartons. Only Heaven knows how many outfits were not sold at retail because of Lionel's ill-conceived packaging concept, one that more often than not left a prospective customer totally in the dark. B. Myles Collection.

VG   LN

Lionel Lines tank car; 3362/64 operating log car; 6059 red M St. L SP-type caboose; 8 curved, 3 straight, 6149, 1025 transformer.

Contents: The outfit box was a Type D display style with 1965 graphics and unboxed components. The rolling stock came with late AAR trucks and had one fixed and one operating coupler. The freight roster was mediocre at best, but the uncatalogued 635 is a collectible engine. Diesel outfits stir collector interest far more than most of their steam counterparts. A. Vincent, F. Davis and E. Reising Collections.   **200   425**

19441   1965

Contents: 237 steam locomotive; 243W square whistle tender; 6014 white Frisco boxcar; 6465 orange Lionel Lines tank car; 6076 red Lehigh Valley hopper; 6059 red M St. L SP-type caboose; 8 curved, 3 straight, 6149, 147 whistle controller, 1025 transformer.

Comments: The outfit box was a Type D display style with 1965 graphics and unboxed contents. The rolling stock was run-of-the-mill 1965 items; but at least it offered a whistle tender which was not the norm for promotional sets. This set was probably assembled simply to deplete inventory on the 237. It was a frequent uncatalogued set component, but also headed a catalogued set in 1963 and 1964, and was available, along with a whistle tender, for separate sale in 1965 and 1966. Reported to B. Greenberg, collector unknown.

   100   200

19444   1965

Contents: 215P/212T Santa Fe Alco AA units; 6176 gray Lehigh Valley hopper; 6142 green gondola with canisters; 6465 orange Lionel Lines tank car; 6130 Santa Fe work caboose; 12 curved, 3 straight, 6149, 90° crossing, 1025 transformer.

Comments: The outfit box was a Type D display style with 1965 graphics and unboxed contents. The rolling stock had late AAR trucks with one fixed and one operating coupler. Note the unusual combination of a powered 215 unit with a 212T. This was done because the 215 shell had a weight riveted to the back of the cab for extra traction, and Lionel did not deem it necessary to have a weighted dummy A unit, hence a non-weighted 212 cab on the dummy chassis. The 215 was never catalogued by Lionel and is one of the more collectible pieces in the Santa Fe Alco series. It surfaces as a component of several other sets from the 1965-1966 period. Refer to 1965 Spiegel outfit 5263. V. Bibelot and P. Ambrose Collections.

   175   350

VG   LN

19444-502   1965

Contents: 215P/218C Santa Fe Alco AB units; 6465 orange Lionel Lines tank car; 6142 blue gondola with canisters; (3362) unstamped helium tank unloading car; 6017-235 Santa Fe SP-type caboose; 12 curved, 3 straight, 6149, 90° crossing, 1025 transformer.

Comments: Notice the outfit number; it is the same as the preceding entry except for a -502 suffix, which suggests a variation of set 19444. This outfit came in a conventional tan two-tier set box. It contained a Santa Fe B unit instead of the 212T in the above mentioned set, an SP-type caboose rather than a work caboose, and replaced the Lehigh Valley hopper with a helium tank unloading car. Note that the 3362 included with this outfit was completely unstamped. Unstamped examples are known variations, but they usually appear later in the decade. T. Randazzo Collection.   **200   425**

19445   1965

237 steam locomotive; 1060T streamlined tender; 6473 rodeo car; 6176 yellow Lehigh Valley hopper; (6402) gray General-type flatcar with cable reels; 6059 red M St. L SP-type caboose; 8 curved, 3 straight, 6149, 1010 transformer.

Comments: This outfit came with unboxed contents in a Type D display-style box with 1965 graphics. The rolling stock came with late AAR trucks and usually had one fixed and one operating coupler. The 237 was a catalogued engine, but it was also a frequent component of uncatalogued sets. There is little demand among collectors for common equipment, even in set form, unless it is in near Mint condition. Reported by T. Klaassen.

   75   150

19450   1965

Contents: 1062 steam locomotive; 1062T slope-back tender; 3362/64 operating log car; 6076 gray Lehigh Valley hopper; 6014 white Frisco boxcar; 6059 red M St. L SP-type caboose; 12 curved, 3 straight, 6149, 90° crossing, 1010 transformer.

Comments: If only a 2360 GG-1 came in half as many sets as the 1062. This outfit was headed by the common-as-dust 1062 and included a roster of rolling stock that was prevalent throughout the 1965 product line. The outfit box was a tan conventional two-tier type in which the contents were held in place and protected by cardboard liners. A. Tolli and F. Davis Collections.

   75   150

In the confusion and rapid pace of a train meet, few collectors would even notice 1966 outfit 19583, let alone give it a second look. How sorry they would be because this set contains two "gems." The printed legend states "DIE CAST LOCOMOTIVE WITH HEADLIGHT", and as a pleasant surprise, it is the rare uncatalogued 251 steam engine. Also observe the engineer's hat, of all things, that is pictured in the bottom loop of the Figure 8 track plan! L. Harold Collection.

	VG	LN

19454   1966

Contents: 216P/213T M St. L Alco AA units. Refer to Sears outfit 9835.

19500   1966

Contents: 1062 steam locomotive; 1061T slope-back tender; 6142 blue gondola without load; 6076 black Lehigh Valley hopper; 6167 SP-type caboose; 8 curved, 2 straight, 1010 transformer.

Comments: This "bare bones" outfit came with un-boxed contents in a Type D display-style box with 1965 graphics. The rolling stock came with fixed coupler AAR trucks and/or arch bar trucks. Unfortunately, this outfit is just another example of a low-end steam set paired with nondescript rolling stock, and is a hard resale in the marketplace. Reported by T. Klaassen.   **50   100**

19506   1966

Contents: 215P/212T Santa Fe Alco AA units. Please refer to J. C. Penney outfit 8279 and Spiegel set 5260 from 1966.

19507   1966

Contents: 215P/212T Santa Fe Alco AA units. Please refer to Spiegel set 5260 from 1966.

19542   1966

Contents: 1062 steam locomotive. See Ward listing for outfit 21301.

19544   1966

Contents: 237 steam locomotive. Refer to Ward listing for outfit 21302.

19557   1966

Contents: 1062 steam locomotive. See listing for Sears outfit 9808.

19561   1966

Contents: 635 Union Pacific diesel switcher. Please refer to Sears outfit 9810.

19567-500   1966

Contents: 1062 steam locomotive; 1061T slope-back tender; 6014 white Frisco boxcar; (6176) yellow unstamped hopper; 6142 blue gondola without load; (6406) gray General-type flatcar with gray-bumpered auto; 6167 SP-type caboose; 18-piece trestle set; "44"-piece railroad accessory set; 12 curved, 10 straight, 1025 transformer.

Comments: If more were better, this would be the best Lionel ever had to offer. The conventional two-tier white outfit box included a label that proclaimed this to be an 87-piece electric train. This was a railroad empire that included the least expensive items available. The engine and rolling stock, except for the 6406 with yellow auto, are of little value to the collector, but the accent pieces place this set in the upper echelon of Lionel un-catalogued collectibles.

The "44"-piece railroad accessory set included with this outfit was numbered "C76591", and was loaded with play value. However, Lionel included a disclaimer stating "The 'cardboard' cut-outs, included in this set, are not

VG LN

manufactured nor are they warranted by the Lionel Toy Corporation". J. Algozzini and P. Iurilli Collections.

550 1300

19569 1966

Contents: 215P/212T Santa Fe Alco AA units; 6142 gondola with canisters; 6050 Swift boxcar; 6176 black Lehigh Valley hopper; 6167 SP-type caboose; 16 curved, 3 straight, 6149, 45° crossing, 1025 transformer.

Comments: This curious outfit came with unboxed contents in a two-tier white conventional set box with a paste-on label identifying the contents and titled "Pretzel Twin Diesel Freight Train". The label covered the entire surface on one end of the box. The roster of contents closely resembles those of outfits 19444 and 19506. Kindly refer to those outfits for additional comments. B. Myles and M. Visnick Collections. **200 375**

19583 1966

Contents: 251 steam locomotive; 1062T slope-back tender; 6142 blue gondola with canisters; 6014 white

VG LN

Frisco boxcar; (6176) black Lehigh Valley hopper; 6167 SP-type caboose; Lionel railroad cap; 12 curved, 4 straight, 1008 camtrol, 90° crossing, 1025 transformer.

Comments: The tender, rolling stock and caboose are unimpressive, but the rare uncatalogued die-cast 251 engine is a prized collector item. The outfit box was a white conventional two-tier style. The roster of contents was printed on a label affixed to one end of the set box, and specific mention is made of an engineer's hat! L. Harold Collection. **350 750**

19586 1966

Contents: 237 steam locomotive; 242T streamlined tender; 6142 green gondola with canisters; (6076) black Lehigh Valley hopper; 6822 night crew searchlight car; 6167 SP-type caboose; 12 curved, 7 straight, 6149, 90° crossing, 1025 transformer.

Comments: What makes this set extremely interesting is a large descriptive sticker that was affixed to the top of the outfit lid, proclaiming "EXCITING G. C. MURPHY EXCLUSIVE BY LIONEL"; in the 1950s it would have been anathema to mention Lionel and G. C. Murphy

This is a rare 219 Missouri Pacific Alco set from 1959 (see listing on page 120). By collector standards, the outfit box was spectacular, but unlike Gifts Galore set X617, there was no set number on the box! Note the sixteen-piece partial trestle set that is stored in the upside down, stepped pyramid shape that was die cut into the center of the filler. We are sure that "something" is missing from the lower center area, but at this time, we haven't a clue as to what it might be. M. Nicholas Collection.

This is THE Halloween General outfit, not Sears set 9666 as has been erroneously listed in other publications. It is dated to 1960, but unfortunately, we cannot list an outfit number because it was not printed on the set box. Note the unique box for the Plasticville Frontier set that was numbered "963-100". Halloween General components appear regularly in the marketplace, but the outfit box is truly rare. The 1882 General engine and tender, along with the 1887 flatcar with horses, were available at the original Madison Hardware to "preferred" customers into the 1980s. J. Algozzini Collection.

	VG	LN

in the same breath. The set box was a 1965 Type D display style. The rolling stock came with varying truck and coupler combinations. Notice that Lionel included what was by 1966 standards a premium car with this set, namely the 6822 searchlight. It was retailed at $8 for separate sale and was still in the process of being depleted as per the listing in the 1969 catalogue! D. Pickard Collection.
125   250

19706   1967

Contents: 215P/212T Santa Fe Alco AA units; 6465 orange Lionel Lines tank car; 6473 rodeo car; 6076 Lehigh Valley hopper; 6059 red M St. L SP-type caboose; 12 curved, 3 straight, 6149, 90° crossing, 1025 transformer.

Comments: This set came with unboxed contents in a plain tan conventional two-tier outfit box. The rolling stock was run-of-the-mill merchandise from the 1966 product line. The listing for outfit 19444 has additional comments on the 215 engine.

Most interestingly, this outfit was also retailed over the counter at select Sears stores in 1967. The authors have verified an example with a miniature Sears price sticker which lists the Sears inventory control number as "9732" and shows the retail price as "$32.99". P. Catalano and R. Spell Collections.
175   325

	VG	LN

19733   1967

Contents: 635 Union Pacific diesel switcher. See Sears listing for outfit 9724.

19806   1968

Contents: 215P/212T Santa Fe Alco AA units; two 2409 Santa Fe Pullmans; 2410 Santa Fe observation car; 8 curved, 4 straight, 1073 transformer.

Comments: Look what we have here—a Santa Fe passenger set that was similar to 1966 Lionel catalogued outfit 11590. Just like set 11590, this outfit came in a Type D display-style box, but note that the powered unit was a 215 and that this set included two Pullmans. Apparently Lionel's supply of Vista Domes was exhausted, but they still owned two-year-old inventory on Pullmans and observation cars. There also seemed to be a glut of 215 engines as the 215 headed an inordinate amount of uncatalogued sets. R. Okun Collection.
350   700

19910   1969

Contents: 1062 (2-4-2) steam locomotive; 1062T slope-back tender; 6142 green gondola with canisters;

This photo shows top and end views of two boxes used for the 963 Plasticville Frontier set. The example shown on top, in a unique box with a western scene, was numbered "963-100" (see end view shown on lower right); it was a component of the Halloween General set only. The other example (box top shown in middle of photo) came in a Classic Lionel box and was numbered only "963" (see end view on bottom left). The Frontier Set, as number 963, was available at $2 for separate sale in the 1959 and 1960 Lionel catalogues, and was also a component of 1959 Sears General set 9666. J. Algozzini Collection.

	VG	LN

(6402) gray General-type flatcar with cable reels; 6176 black Lehigh Valley hopper car; 6059 red M St. L SP-type caboose; 8 curved, 2 straight, 1025 transformer.

Comments: The outfit box was a Type D display style (vintage 1966) that was used in 1969! This set was very similar to catalogued outfit 11710 but included an extra car. This example was sold through Western Auto and retailed for $14.95. Although this outfit has minimal dollar value, it may hold some sentimental fascination because it was near the "bitter end" of Lionel production. W. Grimes Collection.

	75	150

Number Unknown — **1959**

Contents: 219 Missouri Pacific Alco AA units; 6175 flatcar with rocket; 6801 flatcar with boat; 6014-100 Airex boxcar; 6017 SP-type caboose; 12 curved, 3 straight, partial trestle set, 6029, 1015 transformer.

An advanced collector would be overjoyed to find this rare bubble-pack floor sample of an unknown Lionel outfit. This example came on a thick cardstock sheet that was stapled along the perimeter. Note the holes that are present near the tops of the first and last "L" in Lionel; they were used to hang this display sample on a wall. A display such as this allowed a prospective customer to visualize what was included in the tan nondescript Lionel outfit boxes stacked nearby, or available from the stock room. Surely other miscellaneous items were included in the outfit box to account for the 33 pieces mentioned. C. Hurschik Collection.

	VG	LN

Comments: The 219 Missouri Pacific Alcos were not catalogued by Lionel; however, the road name was catalogued on an Alco pair as "205" in 1957 and 1958. This is an outfit for which we cannot provide a number because it did *not* appear on the box. The set box was unique, and similar in concept to what had been used on Gifts Galore outfit X617 and on the Halloween General set from 1960

The track and sixteen-piece partial trestle set allowed for an over-and-under Figure 8 plan. All components fit into uniquely shaped die-cut slots. The 6175 and 6801 were routine production items, but the -100 red Airex boxcar was not catalogued by Lionel. **450 1100**

Number Unknown   1960

Contents: 1882 Halloween General; 1882T tender; 1866 mail/baggage car; 1885 passenger car; 1887 flatcar with horses; 963-100 Plasticville Frontier set; 12 curved, 4 straight, 90° crossing, 1015 transformer.

Comments: This is one of the "premier" postwar promotional outfits; unfortunately, as with the preceding outfit, we cannot list an outfit number because it was *not printed* on the set box! However, this is *THE* Halloween

General set; it was *not* Sears outfit 9666 that has been listed in other literature because it differs in virtually every respect (refer to set 9666 in the Sears chapter). The set box was an oversized maroon flat pack without a lid that included a die-cut filler with red and green sparkles which fit into a plain tan nondescript cardboard sleeve. To afford additional protection, the contents were covered with a piece of flexible gray corrugated cardstock. One example observed by the authors had a retail price of $19.95 written on the set carton in black crayon. A master (or shipping) carton into which a single outfit was placed has also been observed. This set contained a unique Plasticville box for the 963-100 Frontier set that pictured a western scene on the lid, while the 1866 was a regular production item and a component of all other O27 Gauge catalogued General sets. On the other hand, the blue 1885 and the 1887 were common only to this outfit. Extra scrutiny must be given to the flatcar; it is numbered "1887", not "1877", and must come with yellow fencing. Someone in the collecting community must have a flyer or brochure on this set. We are most anxious for additional comments. J. Algozzini, P. Adler and A. Stewart Collections. **1500 3500**

VG   LN

Number Unknown   1963

Contents: 1061 steam locomotive; (1061T) un-stamped slope-back tender; (6406) maroon General-type flatcar with gray-bumpered auto; 6042 blue gondola with cable reels; (6167) red unstamped SP-type caboose; two red canisters; 8 curved, 1026 transformer.

Comments: The items listed above came on a thick cardstock sheet with bubble-pack display-style packaging. It did not include a set number but was marked "33 Piece LIONEL Electric Train Set". This example came with a dark yellow auto for the 6406 and two green cable reels for the gondola. When viewing the color photograph, note that two extraneous unstamped red canisters were packaged with the set for additional play value.

The set was similar to both 1962 advance catalogue set 11001 and outfit 19244. This bubble-pack example was undoubtedly the retail store floor sample for an as yet unidentified set to show a potential customer what was actually enclosed in the sealed, nondescript tan boxes stored in the back room or stacked on nearby shelves. Some other items *had* to be included with this set to justify the "33" pieces mentioned. Possibilities include a cardstock punch-out sheet (see outfit 19328) or a packet of Plasticville yard signs. Outfit 11450, catalogued by Lionel in 1964, is another example of a set known to exist in bubble-style packaging. C. Hurschik Collection.

350   900

GLOSSARY

A unit: lead unit for certain diesel locomotive designs, such as F-3 units; has cab for crew.

AA: combination of two A unit diesel locomotives.

AAR trucks: trucks designed by the Association of American Railroads; Lionel's plastic version was introduced in 1957.

AB: combination of an A and B unit.

ABA: combination of an A unit, a B unit, and a second A unit.

advance catalogue: a catalogue for wholesale and retail distributors that indicated what would most likely be available for sale.

Alco: an acronym for American Locomotive Company, manufacturer of locomotives for full-size railroads; made the FA units popularized in O27 by Lionel.

arch bar truck: the inexpensive plastic truck that was developed for the General components in 1959; also the most commonly used truck for inexpensive advance and uncatalogued sets.

ATSF: abbreviation for Atchison, Topeka and Santa Fe.

B & M: abbreviation for Boston and Maine.

B & O: abbreviation for Baltimore and Ohio.

B unit: trailing unit for certain diesel locomotive designs, such as F-3 diesels; has no cab or windshield.

Bakelite: synthetic resin or plastic used in the early manufacture of toy trains; e.g., Madison passenger cars.

bar-end truck: a metal truck in which the side frame is pressed against a bolster that resembles a bar; it replaced the staple-end truck.

bay window caboose: caboose with no cupola, but with extended side windows.

Berkshire: type of steam locomotive with a 2-8-4 wheel arrangement.

box cab: electric-outline locomotive with a rectangular body, such as the 520 introduced in 1956.

bubble pack: a method of packaging in which a thick cardstock sheet is covered by a clear piece of plastic molded in "bubbles" to protect and hold individual items in place.

Budd RDC: self-propelled Rail Diesel Car; resembles a passenger car; modeled by Lionel as 400 and 404.

C & O: abbreviation for Chesapeake and Ohio.

C unit: a term used by Lionel in catalogues and on boxes to identify their B units.

camtrol: plastic track-mounted device for O27 that allows manual uncoupling.

center cab: a rectangular-shaped 44-ton diesel with a center engineer's cab. Lionel's model, introduced in 1956, was grossly out of scale; e.g., 627 Lehigh Valley.

chassis: synonym for frame.

CN: abbreviation for Canadian National.

coach: basic passenger car; usually has windows along entire length of each side.

coil coupler: type of coupler that was activated by a sliding shoe; more costly to manufacture than magnetic couplers.

Columbia: type of steam locomotive with a 2-4-2 wheel arrangement.

combine: car used in passenger trains with combination of uses, such as baggage-passenger combination, or baggage-Railway Post Office combination.

consist: the makeup of a train's rolling stock.

consumer catalogue: a catalogue that was offered to the general public to promote Lionel trains.

couplers: mechanical devices used to connect cars; made in many different variations on toy trains; Lionel used knuckle couplers for postwar production.

crossing: a piece of track that allows one track to pass over another; 45° and 90°; useful for yards, Figure 8s and main line crossings.

die-cast: a term describing a method of manufacturing in which molten metal is forced into a die and cooled, creating an object that takes the shape of the die; e.g., 736 Berkshire boiler.

die-cut: a box or insert cut by mechanical means to make openings for the contents.

drawbar: the hook-like device that attaches a steam engine to its tender.

dummy: non-powered locomotive; for example, the B units in many AB combinations sold by toy train companies were dummies as were non-powered A units.

ECU-1: Electronic Control Unit; a box-like device that was included with the Electronic Sets to control train function.

electrical ground: as specifically used in this book, a copper spring riveted to the front truck of certain tenders. The spring in conjuction with the drawbar is necessary to maintain ground (outside rail) electrical contact to the reversing unit of inexpensive four-wheel locomotives. These locomotives lose ground contact when passing over the non-conducting portions of crossings or switches.

EMD: Electro-Motives Division of General Motors; maker of the F-3.

EP-5: specific type of electric locomotive with a cab on each end; no walkways; e.g., 2350 New Haven.

F-3: specific type of diesel locomotive; rounded nose, no walkways; popularized by Lionel; e.g., 2343 Santa Fe.

FA: specific type of Alco diesel locomotive; eight wheels, rounded nose; popularized in O27 by Lionel; e.g., 2023 Union Pacific.

Fairbanks-Morse (F-M): manufacturer of locomotives for the real railroads; produced the "Trainmaster" made popular by Lionel; e.g., 2321 Lackawanna.

feedwater heater: accessory on a steam locomotive, usually on the boiler front above the headlight; e.g., 665.

fixed coupler: a coupler that does not operate; has components that are fixed in place; either plastic or die-cast.

frame: bottom part of a car or locomotive, to which wheels or trucks are attached.

gauge: distance between the rails; specific names are used to describe the commonly used sizes, such as HO Gauge, O Gauge, Standard Gauge, etc.

GE: abbreviation for General Electric, manufacturer of locomotives for real railroads; Lionel's model of the 44-ton center-cab diesel was based upon a GE design.

Geep: railroader's slang for GP-series locomotives.

GG-1: popular electric locomotive used by the Pennsylvania Railroad; created by famed industrial designer Raymond Loewy; modeled by Lionel and others; e.g., 2332.

GP-7 or GP-9: specific types of diesel locomotives; boxy, walkways around sides; modeled by Lionel; e.g., 2028 Pennsylvania and 2349 Northern Pacific.

ground spring: see electrical ground.

heat-stamped: process of lettering toy trains using heat and colored tape; usually makes a slight impression on plastic or metal surfaces.

Hudson: steam locomotive with a 4-6-4 wheel arrangement. Larger examples such as 773 are referred to as NYC type while smaller Hudsons such as 665 are called Santa Fe type.

injection molding: a process in which liquefied plastic is forced into a mold and then cooled; the plastic takes on the shape of the mold.

lithographed: process of applying paint or ink to sheet metal; commonly used by early toy manufacturers and in the production of early trains; no longer in favor, but continued in usage for low-priced items.

M St. L: abbreviation for Minneapolis and St. Louis.

magnetic coupler: the replacement for the coil coupler; introduced in 1948 and activated by an electromagnet.

Magnetraction: special design element of Lionel locomotives using magnetized components to improve traction (pulling power); introduced in 1949 on 622 and 6220 diesel switchers.

Manumatic: Lionel's trade name for a manual uncoupler; developed for the Scout series introduced in 1948.

MKT: abbreviation for Missouri-Kansas-Texas.

MoPac: abbreviation for Missouri Pacific.

N & W: abbreviation for Norfolk and Western.

Northern: type of steam locomotive with a 4-8-4 wheel arrangement; the 746 N & W was the only Northern that Lionel made during the postwar era.

NW-2: specific type of diesel switcher modeled by Lionel; e.g., 6250 Seaboard.

O27 track: Lionel's lightweight track that is $7/16$" high; eight sections form a circle with a diameter of 27 inches measured from outer rail to outer rail.

O track: Lionel's heavier weight track that is $11/16$" high; eight sections form a circle with a diameter of 31 inches measured from outer rail to outer rail.

observation: passenger car usually used at the end of a train; open platform or rounded end with large windows for "observation" of scenery by passengers.

OPS: Office of Price Stabilization; established in early 1950s in an attempt to control rampant inflation; OPS stickers and stamps showed that stringent pricing guidelines had been issued.

over and under: track layout design that uses trestles to allow the lower level to pass under the upper level.

P unit: designation used for powered diesel locomotives.

Pacific: type of steam locomotive with a 4-6-2 wheel arrangement; Lionel did not make a Pacific engine in the postwar era but used an artist's rendering of one on some early 1960s display-style outfit boxes.

porthole caboose: center-cupola caboose with round porthole windows that was modeled after the Pennsylvania N5C.

powered: refers to a locomotive with a motor; used when necessary to distinguish between an operating locomotive and a dummy unit.

promotion: the selling of goods and/or services through a special program with emphasis placed on a lower price or better value.

promotional set: one assembled to promote the name and/or product of a manufacturer or a retailer. For example, Gifts Galore set X617 promoted only the company name and contained no special item, whereas outfit X-589 promoted the name RCA Whirlpool on a special-issue boxcar.
Also interpreted to mean a set considered by the general buying public to be an exceptional monetary value. Many were assembled by Lionel and offered to retailers simply to promote (sell) overstocked inventory or to utilize factory production capability. Medium-priced uncatalogued sets similar to Lionel catalogued offerings were often sold by various retailers to capitalize on the well-known Lionel trade name.

Pullman: specific type of passenger car originally designed by George Pullman; often used as a generic term for better-grade passenger cars.

RCS: Remote Controlled uncoupling/operating Section without an electromagnet.

rectifier: another term often used in reference to some electric locomotives; commonly used to refer to Lionel's 2329 Virginian.

reefer: slang term for a refrigerator car, such as those used to ship meats and other perishables.

RI: abbreviation for Rock Island.

rolling stock: any railroad car that is not self-propelled, but must be pulled by an engine.

rubber-stamped: process of lettering toy trains using rubber pads.

S & H: abbreviation for Sperry and Hutchinson.

scale: proportion of a model to its prototype; for example, an O scale model is 1/48 actual size; therefore O scale is also referred to as 1/48 or 1:48 scale; most Lionel models were slightly less than scale.

Scout: term that refers to sets or components in sets that included a "Lionel Scout" tender and components with both Scout trucks and couplers; Scout engines include 1001, 1110, and 1120.

Scout-like: term that has come to mean all small, inexpensive engines with an 0-4-0 or 2-4-2 wheel alignment.

Scout-type: term that is interchangeable with "Scout-like."

semi-Scout: term used to describe rolling stock and the 6001T and 6066T tenders that have the combination of Scout trucks and magnetic couplers.

SP: abbreviation for Southern Pacific.

SP-type caboose: Southern Pacific square cupola caboose with cupola oriented towards the rear; introduced in late 1947 and produced with several road names and a variety of trim.

staple-end truck: a metal truck with the side frames attached with what appears to be a staple that is bent outwards.

steam switcher: type of small steam engine with an 0-4-0 wheel arrangement that was used for yard duty, not main line service.

stock car: commonly called a "cattle car"; used for hauling livestock.

streamlined: locomotives, tenders and other trains featuring aerodynamic designs; highly popular in the 1930s.

Super O: Lionel's specialized track system introduced in 1957 that consists of plastic ties with a copper contact strip in place of the third rail; twelve sections form a circle with a diameter of 38 inches measured from outer rail to outer rail.

switch: a track section also called a turnout with movable rails which can transfer a train from one track to another.

switcher: type of light-duty locomotive usually used in railroad yards.

T unit: designation used for trailing or non-powered diesel engines.

tab frame: a cost-saving frame introduced in 1958 for SP-type cabooses. It eliminated the use of screws as a means of attaching the cab to the chassis.

tender: commonly called a "coal car" by non-railroaders; used to haul fuel for a steam locomotive.

three-rail: track system popularized by Lionel; features two outside running rails (electrically grounded) and a single rail along the center that provides the positive current.

tinplate: toys made from tin-coated steel; also used loosely to describe items that are caricatures of real trains rather than scale models.

transformer: the electrical power source for a model train. Lionel manufactured numerous types ranging from a lowly 1011 with 25 watts of power to a high of 275 watts in the ZW model that could run four trains simultaneously.

truck: assembly that mounts the wheels beneath a railroad car.

truss rods: steel support rods used on the underframes of freight and passenger cars on early railroads; once associated with hobos, who slept on the truss rods beneath the cars.

turbine: Lionel's model of the Pennsylvania railroad 6-8-6 S-2 steam turbine.

two-rail: track arrangement similar to that used on the real roads; commonly used by American Flyer (for its S Gauge models) and by most scale model railroad manufacturers.

UCS: uncoupling/operating section of track that allows automatic operation of couplers by means of an electromagnet; replacement for the RCS; introduced in 1949.

uncatalogued set: any outfit that either did not appear or was not offered in Lionel's advance or consumer catalogue.

uncoupler: track-mounted device that allows uncoupling of cars, either manually or by remote control.

unnumbered: term used to describe an item on which no numbers appear, but on which lettering is usually present. The item number has been taken from the *Lionel Service Manual* listing and appears in this book within parentheses; e.g., (6121) flatcar with pipes.

unstamped: a term used to describe an item that is neither lettered nor numbered; the item number has been taken from the *Lionel Service Manual* listing and appears in this book within parentheses.

UP: abbreviation for Union Pacific.

U.S.M.C.: abbreviation for United States Marine Corp.

INDEX

Outfit	Page	Outfit	Page	Outfit	Page	Outfit	Page
6P4803	72	1119	88	2211WS	24	5940	23, 25, (25)
6P-4810	92	1403	23	2217WS	24	5946	23
6P-4811	(108), 110	1403W	23	2225WS	24	5950	23
6P4811	(107), (108),	1405W	23	2275W	66	5951	23
	109, (109 box), 110	1423W	23	2277WS	66	5954	23
11-L-19	66	1427WS	23	2281W	66	5955	23
11-L-40	66	1431	23	2285W	66	5958	23
11-L-41	66, (67)	1431W	23	2529W	66	5960	23
11-L-42	66, (70 box)	1435WS	23	2893	94, (94)	5961	23
11-L-51	66, 67	1451WS	23	3000	44, 45	5966	23
11-L-53	66	1453WS	23	3001	44, 45	5967	23
11-L-55	66	1461S	23	3002	44, 45	5970	23
11-L-56	66	1463W	23	3003	44, 45	5976	23
11-L-58	66	1463WS	23	3004	44, 46	5977	23
11-L-59	66	1465	23	3018	44, 46	5980	23
11-L-60	66	1467W	23	3019	44, 46	5981	23
11-L-62	66	1469WS	23	3030	44, 46	5982	23
11-L-63	66	1477S	23	3031	44, 46	5985	23
11-L-64	66	1479WS	23	3048	44, 46	5987	23
11-L-256	66	1485WS	23	3049	44, 47	8261	57, 64
11-L-259	66	1500	24	3053	44, 47	8279	57, (63), 64
108-105	99, (99)	1501	24	3058	44, 47	8287	57, 64
149	70, (70)	1503WS	24	3073	44, 47	9601	23
505X	23, 26	1505WS	24	3074	44, 47	9602	23, 26
0664	57, 58, (58)	1513S	24	3100 Series	69	9603	23
0672	57, 58	1517W	24	3103W	88	9606	23, 26
0680	(38), 57, 59, (59)	1520W	66	3700	57, 60	9613	23
700	66	1523	24	3718	57, 60	9640	23, 26
702	66	1527	23	3726	57, 61, (61)	9641	23, 26
725	66	1533WS	23	3734	57, 62, (62)	9642	23, 26
728	66	1542	66	4782	57, 62	9643	23, 26
731	66	1543	24, 66	4881	57, 63	9651	23
733	66	1547S	66, (70 box)	4899	57, 63	9652	23, 26, 27, (27)
735	66	1553W	23	5258	50, 51	9653	23, 28
750	66	1569	66	5259	50, 51	9654	23, 28
815	66	1575	66	5260	50, 51	9655	23, 29
817	66	1579S	66	5261	50, 51	9656	23, 29, (28), 30
819	66	1583WS	66	5262	50, 51	9657	23, (29), 30
821	66	1586	66	5263	50, 52	9658	23, 24, 30
1000W	23	1615	66	5266	50, 53	9659	24, 30
1001	23	2058	88, (88 box)	5276	50, 54	9661	24, 31
1082	57, 60	2105WS	23	5277	50, 54	9662	24
1090	57, 60, (60 box)	2125WS	23	5278	50, (52), 54	9664	24, 31
1100 Series	69	2137WS	23	5284	50, (53), 54,	9665	24, 31
1112	23, 25, (25)	2147WS	23		(54 box)	9666	24, (31), 32
1115	86, (87), (87 box)	2173WS	23	5285	50, 54	9668	24
1117	23	2187WS	24	5286	50, 55	9670	24, 32
				5287	50, 55	9671	24
				5939	23	9672	24, 32

( ) — indicates a photograph

127

Outfit	Page	Outfit	Page	Outfit	Page	Outfit	Page
9673	24, 32	19142-100	95, (96)	19439	115	X 100 Series	69
9675	24, 32	19142-502	95, (97)	19440	(111), 115	X-150	70, (71)
9682	24, 32	19147	96	19441	116	X 200 Series	69
9683	24, 33	19185	(52), 54, 97	19444	(112), 116	X 300 Series	69
9687	24	19200 Series	69	19444-502	(113), 116	X 400 Series	69
9692	24, 33, (33)	19203X	97	19445	116	X-400	66, 67, 71
9693	24, 33	19212	98	19450	(114), 116	X-444	71
9694	24, 34	19216	98, (98)	19454	24, 117	X 500 Series	69
9723	24, 34	19219	99, (99)	19500	117	X 500 NA Series	69
9724	24, 35	19220	99	19500 Series	69	X-516NA	72
9730	24, 35	19225	100, (100)	19506	(63), 64, 117	X-526NA	72
9732	24	19228	101, (101)	19507	51, 117	X-531NA	72
9745(A)	88, (89)	19244	102	19542	47, (48 box), 117	X-532NA	73, (73)
9745(B)	89	19247	102	19544	48, 117	X-533NA	73
9745(C)	90, (90)	19260	(102), 103	19557	24, 35, (36 box), 117	X-544NA	73
9745(D)	90	19260-500	103	19561	24, 35, 117	X-550NA	75
9807	24, 35	19262	103, (103)	19567-500	(115), 117	X-556	75
9808	24, 35, (36 box)	19263	104, (104)	19569	(115 box), 118	X-568NA	(74), 76
9810	24, 35	19281	(105), (105 box), 106	19583	(117 box), 118	X573NA	(75 box), 76
9813	24, (36), 37			19586	118	X-579NA	76
9820	24, 37, (37), (38)	19300 Series	69	19600 Series	69	X-580NA	77
9834	24, 39, (39) (40 box)	19325	24, (36,) 37, 107	19700 Series	69	X-584NA	77
9835	24, 39	19328	(106), 108	19706	24, 119	X-589	(76), 77
9836	24, 41	19333	58, (58), 109	19733	24, (34), 35, 119	X 600 Series	69
10600 Series	69	19334	(38), 59, (59), 109	19800 Series	69	X600	77, (78)
10613 SF	91, (91)	19341	109	19806	119	X-610NAA	77, (79)
10653 SF	92	19350	(107), 109	19900 Series	69	X617	78, (80), (81 box)
10663 SF	92	19350-500	(108), (109 box), 110	19910	119	X-619	78, (81 box)
11331	92	19351-500	(110), 111	21301	44, 47, (48 box)	X640	79, (82)
11540-500	92	19371	(53), 54, 111	21302	44, 48	X-643	80, (83)
11570	92	19394	112	DX 837	85, (86)	X-646	82
11600 Series	69	19400 Series	69	Halloween General	(119), (120 box), 121	X-654	82
11620	92, (93)	19427	112	Number Unknown	(118), (119), (121), 120, 121, 122	X 700 Series	69
12885	24	19428	113			X714	83, (84), (85)
19000	94, (94)	19436	113			X-714	83
19000 Series	69	19437	61, (61), 114			X 800 Series	69
19100 Series	69	19438	62, (62), 114			X 800 NA Series	69
19110	94, (95)	19438-502	114			X-802	84
19142	95					X-821NA	85
						X-875	86

( ) — indicates a photograph